"Donald Hook has written an absorbing account of growing up in Lynchburg during the Great Depression and World War II. *Back Then—Those Were the Days* will undoubtedly call up a multitude of memories for today's senior citizens. Their children and grandchildren—the Baby Boom and younger generations—will discover a Hill City bereft of most of the conveniences they take for granted in the twenty-first century and perhaps wonder how their elders ever survived those difficult years."

—James M. Elson, editor,
Lynch's Ferry, A Journal of Local History

"Having grown up in the same part of Lynchburg as the author, I share many fond memories of people, places, and events he describes in *Back Then—Those Were the Days*. A personal narrative like this one seems much more effective in portraying what everyday life was really like than the more objective approach of the professional historian."

—T. Gibson Hobbs, Jr., historian and
founding member of the *Lynch's Ferry* editorial board

Back Then—Those Were the Days is an informative chronicle of a childhood spent in the South during the Great Depression. Donald Hook portrays an era before television and computers when freedom and self-sufficiency were really more available to children. Viewed through the eyes of a child struggling into manhood, Lynchburg provides a setting which will be familiar to those who lived it and marvelous to anyone who has only heard about it.

—Thomas G. Ledford, administrator,
Lynchburg Museum

Back Then—Those Were the Days

Recollections of a Boy Growing Up During the Depression

Back Then—Those Were the Days

Recollections of a Boy Growing Up During the Depression

Donald D. Hook

Unlimited Publishing
Bloomington, Indiana

Distributing Publisher:
Unlimited Publishing LLC
Bloomington, Indiana

http://www.unlimitedpublishing.com

Contributing Publisher: Donald D. Hook

Cover and book design by Charles King. Copyright © 2003 by Unlimited Publishing LLC. This book was typeset with Adobe® InDesign®, using the Adobe Garamond®, Myriad®, and Adobe Jensen® typefaces. This book makes use of one or more typefaces specifically licensed by and customized for the exclusive use of Unlimited Publishing LLC.

Unlimited Publishing LLC provides worldwide book design, printing, marketing and distribution services for professional writers and small to mid-size presses, serving as distributing publisher. Sole responsibility for the content of each work rests with the author(s) and/or contributing publisher(s). The opinions expressed herein may not be interpreted in any way as representing those of Unlimited Publishing, nor any of its affiliates.

To receive a signed paperback copy of this book, send $12 by check or money order (includes S&H, no sales tax in Delaware) with your name and mailing address to: Dr. D. D. Hook, P.O. Box 1682, Millsboro, DE 19966-1682. Expect delivery within 6-8 weeks.

First edition.

Copies of this book and others
are available to order online at:

http://www.unlimitedpublishing.com/authors

ISBN 1-58832-079-0 (Hardback)
ISBN 1-58832-080-4 (Paperback)

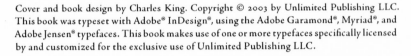

Unlimited Publishing
Bloomington, Indiana

To my parents, who would remember even more
if they were still around:

Dwight Carlisle Hook (1896-1975)
and
Eunice Fowler Hook (1897-1995)

Formerly Bragassa's (see p. 37), now the temporary home of the
Lynchburg Museum, normally located in the old Court House

List of Illustrations

Acknowledgments

I wish to acknowledge the kind and thorough assistance provided by Dr. James M. Elson, editor, *Lynch's Ferry* magazine, and Mr. T. Gibson Hobbs, Jr., historian and civic-minded citizen, in preparing the first draft of the manuscript. Their courtesy, attention to detail, and promptness of response will long be remembered. Whereas Lynchburg was my home only for about the first decade and a half of my life and has been Jim Elson's only for the last decade and a half, Gibson Hobbs is a more genuine Lynchburger than either of us, for not only is he a native who stayed put, his father was one as well. It was comforting to discover that my memory was seldom in disagreement with theirs.

Thanks are also due Mr. Phillip Wayne Rhodes, Director of the Jones Memorial Library, for making available certain photographs from the library's collection, which are listed above, to Mr. Thomas Ledford of the Lynchburg Museum System for reading the manuscript, and to Mrs. Nancy Blackwell Marion of The Design Group for reading the manuscript and providing two pictures listed and credited above.

Contents

Panorama of Lynchburg, *Va.*, with Williams Viaduct

Preface

❧The events and people in this book are centered in a small city called Lynchburg, in the southwestern part of Virginia. The time is that of the Great Depression, the years 1929 through 1939, with a carryover through the years of World War II. The experiences are those of the author, born in the 1920s and growing up in Lynchburg during the 1930s and 1940s. The book is narrated in the third person in the hope of conveying at least the semblance of objectivity. It is also hoped this book will be seen for what it really is: the experiences of *one* person, but reflective of those of many who grew up throughout the United States and elsewhere in the western world in those crucial years.

Lynchburg is an historic city. Clearly recognizing the need for a better means of crossing the James River than a mere fording place at what is now the foot of 9th Street, John Lynch began operation of a ferry service a few hundred yards upstream in 1757. It immediately became successful and led Lynch to petition the General Assembly of Virginia in 1784 for a charter for a town beginning at that spot. Two years later the charter founding Lynchburg was granted.

From that village, leading up to a hill overlooking the ferry site, Lynchburg began to grow. By 1805 it was incorporated as a town. Businesses included tobacco warehouses, blacksmith shops, and dry goods and grocery stores. By the end of the 1830s the town's population was close to 6000, and by 1852 Lynchburg was designated a city. By 1880, there were more than 15,000 people living there. During the Depression years the population remained at approximately 41,000. During all this time Lynchburg gradually evolved from a tobacco-based economy into a regional manufacturing center. Thus, the foundation was laid for an economy that largely withstood the ravages of the Great Depression. Since World War II the city has steadily undergone modernization and diversification. Today there are more than 66,000 people residing in and around the city.

There has long been a catchy phrase associated with the city of Lynchburg, "The City on Seven Hills," those hills being College, Daniel's, Diamond, Federal, Franklin, Garland, and White Rock. The term "Hill City" is also frequently heard and used in business names. Federal Hill designated the earliest wealthy section and was followed by Diamond Hill, later by Rivermont, Peakland, and Boonsboro. Each of the other "hill" sections was class-distinctive and, as in all cities that have survived into the present century, eventually waned as each aged. The downtown has suffered the same fate as malls have sprung up in predominantly residential areas. Several of the places where the author worked are no longer there, and their recollection evokes nostalgia.

There are many cities in the United States and throughout the world known as "The City on Seven Hills." Among them is Cincinnati, named after the Society of Cincinnati, formed in 1783 by former Revolutionary officers and harking back to the Roman dictator Cincinnatus (458 & 439 B.C.). Of course, only one city has been known for more than 2000 years as the City on Seven Hills: Rome. We can precisely name those hills: Aventine, Capitoline, Celian, Esquitine, Palatine, Quirinal, Viminal. Istanbul, almost as old, also claims seven hills. So does much newer Nevada City, California. Some there have romantically descriptive names such as Piety Hill, Lost Hill, and Nabob Hill. Even Rome, Georgia, is built on seven hills.

Unlike the hills of the better-known places above, which more often laid claim to individual fame, Lynchburg's hills mostly tended to isolate urban elements from each other and the city from much of the surrounding countryside. In fact, Lynchburg has remained an independent city since its founding. To some, this isolation has seemed a distinct disadvantage, making Lynchburg far too insular socially and intellectually. That may be true, but its isolation and inborn self-reliance helped to rescue it from the clutches of the Great Depression.

In relatively recent years the United States has undergone a number of recessions. Although not unaware of the financial hardships experienced by some, as one who lived through the entire Great Depression, I have often compared these minor events or "market corrections," as they have sometimes been euphemistically described, with "the real thing" and found them related but not comparable.

There have been periods of boom and bust throughout the 19th and 20th centuries, as well as the recurring market uncertainties of the 21st century. I surely do not wish to make light of the stock market crash of October 1987, but nothing in all that time has equaled the long-term effects of the 10 years of the Great Depression, 1929-1939. Not to be overlooked is the dreadful weather throughout that decade—frigid, snowy winters, unbearable heat, drought, floods, and grasshoppers.

Roughly, in another decade death will have claimed the last of those for whom the Depression was once a day-to-day reality. Even those living now who never actually experienced it first-hand, as well as their progeny, will continue to feel its icy hand for years to come. Though by no means exhaustive of my experiences, this book attempts to stir up recollections in the minds of people of my generation so that they may be induced to read or augment these or transmit similar stories and impressions to their children and grandchildren for safekeeping.

—Donald D. Hook

The Author, Charlotte, North Carolina

CHAPTER I

In the Beginning—and Before

In writing most books it is hard to know where to begin. Often it is just as difficult to know when to stop. However, when you are writing a book about yourself, the first task is pretty easy: Start with your birth. But since you can't write when you are dead, that business of when to end the book is still a problem!

Actually, for Donald, knowing when to begin was harder than for most because he could recall things and places before his birth in 1928 even though he couldn't remember the event as such. He knows that sounds crazy, but he "proved" it to his mother on several occasions by recalling the appearance of a house the family lived in before he was born and for several months thereafter. He could even describe the street. It was unpaved and dusty, and the house looked like one of those 1920s bungalows with the sloping front roof and a hedge out front. And there were no pictures of the house and street to tip him off. Of course, such early observations were dismissed by all as nonsense.

It was well before any camera technically more advanced than the Brownie box camera was readily obtainable and long before clairvoyants, mystics, and other "hysterics" were taken more seriously than Ouija boards. Donald's father told him years later that he was a sickly baby at birth and that the attending physician had put him up on a shelf in the birthing room of St. Peter's Hospital in Charlotte, North Carolina, thinking this new citizen wasn't going to make it. Well, he did.

As for memories of past events, Donald retained many—from nursing his mother to recalling details of houses the family lived in over his childhood years. Why he can't call to mind the first apartments they occupied in Richmond and Lynchburg, Virginia—on Court Street, he was told—after moving up from Charlotte in 1930, he can't say.

But he does remember the first house in Lynchburg, a duplex on Warwick Lane, maybe mainly because that is when he got the mumps and the health department nailed an ominous yellow and black and white pentagonal sign on the house, to the right of the front door, and stamped it QUARANTINED. There were to be no visitors for two weeks, and he was confined pretty much to his bedroom. Not a very nice deal for an energetic two-year-old!

In those days children didn't receive a whole series of shots as infants; in fact, it was hoped they would have at least a sub-clinical case of the measles and mumps so they would acquire a later immunity. For boys it was especially good to have mumps early so as not to risk sterility from an infection contracted as an adult. It wasn't until 1934 or 1935, after he had started school, that Donald received diphtheria and typhoid shots. Getting shots never bothered him, and he was both annoyed and amused at the fit the other kids put on when the school nurse made everybody line up to "get stuck."

Then there was the brick apartment house just across the little cross street to the left of Donald's house at 218 Warwick Lane where Maggie and Mr. Hudgins lived on the second floor. They were a friendly, young, childless couple who doted on Donald. When he visited them with his mother, he could play with his top and truck right in the middle of their living room floor and get everybody's attention, something every child laps up. (It is ironic that, some 16 years later, Donald and Calvin Hudgins worked for competing funeral homes. Mr. Hudgins was a funeral director at Diuguid's, and later established his own mortuary.)

But some kinds of attention he wished to avoid. One day he lost a battle with his mother, who had pestered him to sing a solo standing in front of a bunch of her lady friends in the Hudginses' apartment. It was awful—the solo as well as the experience, though everybody clapped. It was the sort of thing children were always expected to do in those days when company was around. Otherwise, they were supposed to be quiet and practically invisible. The reliance on self-made music back then—piano and voice—virtually assured every child some performance misery from time to time. If it was discovered the kid had taken dancing lessons, the cruelty was compounded. Of course, there were always some kids who thrived on exhibitionism. Donald was not one of them.

Once Donald's mother had to go to the hospital for some reason, and one of her younger sisters, Winnie, came all the way from Georgia to look after him. One day Winnie accidentally slammed the Hudginses' car door shut on his right-hand index finger. Boy, did that ever hurt! She immediately took him to a doctor's office downtown. He vividly remembers to this day seeing his finger, which appeared to be in two pieces, being swirled around in a metal dish full of some green liquid. Then Dr. Hopkins somehow put the pieces together and wrapped up the injured finger in a huge bandage. (Thirty years later that same pediatrician sewed up Donald's son's head after the youngster had fallen off the back of a chair at his grandparents' house and struck a radiator!) Dr. Hopkins told Winnie that she or Donald's mother should bring him back in a week for a checkup and a fresh bandage.

Winnie carried Donny—that's what she always called him—to the hospital to see his mother. He was proudly holding up his bandaged hurt finger, but Winnie was crying and saying to Donny's mother how sorry she was that this had to happen when she was given charge. Of course, nobody really blamed her, but she talked about it for years.

Maybe to show that he didn't blame her either, Donny went with Winnie—he held her hand all the way—for her to get married just two days later. Her fiancé, John Howard, who had just landed a fine job with an insurance company and who was feeling very lonely down in Georgia, had driven all the way to Virginia and asked her to marry him. Winnie didn't hesitate. The three of them climbed umpteen outdoor steps leading from Church Street up to the court house on Court Street in Lynchburg, where a judge performed the ceremony. All his life Donny remembered standing there in that courtroom holding Winnie's hand while she and John answered a lot of questions he didn't understand. Life was already acquiring both an interesting and a confusing side.

Of course, the stock market crash of October 1929 brought forth no sudden reaction from a one-year-old child, but neither did it, surprisingly, from most of the populace. There were indeed people who had lost all their investments and in despair jumped out of high buildings in New York City, and there were others who wrote disconsolate notes and took their lives in other ways and in other places, but they represented a very small fraction of the American people. Maybe no more than five percent of the American people held stocks at that time. Some people, even Charles Poor Kindleberger, author of the classic *The World in Depression*, who was a college sophomore at the time, by his own admission, hardly noticed, or understood, what had happened. The effects of the crash were like a slow seepage affecting different persons at different ages, different sections of the country at different times, and different countries for different reasons until the whole world fell victim one way or the other.

Monument Terrace

2800 Rivermont Avenue

CHAPTER 2

First Impressions

ঐIt must have been sometime in the late fall of 1930 or early 1931 that the family moved to 2800 Rivermont Avenue. Once again, the building was a duplex, but not a side-by-side type. This apartment was spacious and took up the entire ground floor. Upstairs was another apartment, in which lived a couple named Abrahams from North Carolina who had a little daughter by the name of Nina Eve. She and Donny immediately became playmates because, for one thing, there weren't any other children around and, for another thing, being younger, she would do everything Donny asked her to. (See the photo on page 8.) Nina Eve's mother only wished her daughter would obey her as well as she did Donny. Nina Eve loved to jump vigorously up and down on her bed—or any bed, for that matter—as if it were a trampoline, until the bed was a complete and utter mess. For a while her mother tolerated this wild behavior, but when the slats fell out of the bed and it collapsed and broke one day, fun and games were over, and a lecture about what things cost was delivered at length. Donny was there and took it all in. He had heard similar sermons from his mother about the cost of things.

The house had a spacious front yard and was situated on a corner, with a couple hundred feet of sidewalk in the front and along one side, an absolutely ideal place to ride one's tricycle. You could come roaring down the slightly sloping front yard and careen onto the sidewalk or simply pedal majestically up and down, back and forth, on the concrete. (See the photo on page 10.) Until she got her own tricycle, Donny would let Nina Eve stand on the

Nina Eve and the author

back of his. It didn't matter that she fell off sometimes; she wasn't a cry baby and her mother wasn't one of the cautious sort. There were no helmets for trike or bike riders, children or adults. The two children never ventured into the street, although it wouldn't have been particularly dangerous. After all, in those days there wasn't very much traffic!

Donny would actually have liked much more traffic, for he loved all kinds of vehicles. His greatest evening pleasure was to sit in the front yard with his parents and Nina Eve and her parents and identify the various makes of automobiles passing by. There was not a single make he could not recognize by sight or sound. In fact, he was so good at listening, in the dark or with closed eyes or head turned away, to the sound of a car's engine and proclaiming its manufacturer and year that the grown-ups made a game of it and challenged him to name as many out of ten as he could. He never missed. He could easily distinguish a Ford from a Chevrolet, a Buick from a Chrysler, a 1929 Packard from a 1931, or even a Dodge from a Huppmobile, just by the sound of its engine. Later, he was able to do the same with airplanes, of which there were, of course, not all that many back then. (See the photo on page 12.)

Life was pretty good for Donny despite the Depression. The house and yard were nicer than what most people had, and, after losing several jobs, his father had finally landed a good and permanent position with the big H. J. Heinz Company. Only trouble was he had to travel a lot, and that meant that Donny and his mother had to rely on the streetcar for transportation when they couldn't go somewhere on foot, say, to the grocery store.

Donny had only one major disappointment while on Rivermont Avenue, and that was the time his traveling father failed to bring back from his territory the long-promised bulb horn for Donny's tricycle. This was a necessary accessory, you understand, because, as he explained to his parents, ladies out walking on the avenue were afraid Donny would run over them. He needed a loud horn to blow in order to announce his presence.

The author on his tricycle

Well, after his father forgot the horn the first time and saw the disappointment in his son's eyes, he brought home a really big and impressively loud one the following week. Some of the old ladies nearly jumped out of their shoes when they heard the squeeze-blasts from Donny's horn. Within a year, the tricycle was replaced first by a scooter, then by a bicycle, and the horn by a bell on the handlebars. The law said bicycles were to be ridden only in the street, but nobody but fussy old ladies minded if kids tore up and down the sidewalk.

He was pretty young all right, but Donny was already beginning to witness the disappointment of others and, worse, see evidence of hunger around him during those Depression years when so many were out of work. By 1932 the situation was really bad. Several times a week different men would appear at the back door and offer to do some chore for a sandwich and a cup of coffee. It impressed Donny that his mother always provided a little food even if there was no work. Nina Eve's mother would do the same. But for her, it was often a chance to have their big vegetable garden on the next street over cultivated in exchange for fresh vegetables.

At some point Donny began to notice that, though they themselves didn't have an overabundance of food, his family was better off than many. The unkempt men roaming the streets from door to door asking for food or work formed a lasting picture in the child's mind of "The Great Depression" that he was only able to clarify for himself much later. He heard the word "depression" in the conversation of adults almost every day and once saw men in line at a government office or a church when he went downtown. He was told they were waiting for bread or money or some other handout. He noticed that many people were dressed in ragged clothes and smelled like they needed a bath. He was vaguely aware that he had been born merely a decade after the end of the so-called Great War, the "War to End All Wars," now known as World War I; that his father had served in it; and that it had somehow led up to "the stock market crash of 1929," whatever that was, consequently putting a lot of people out of work.

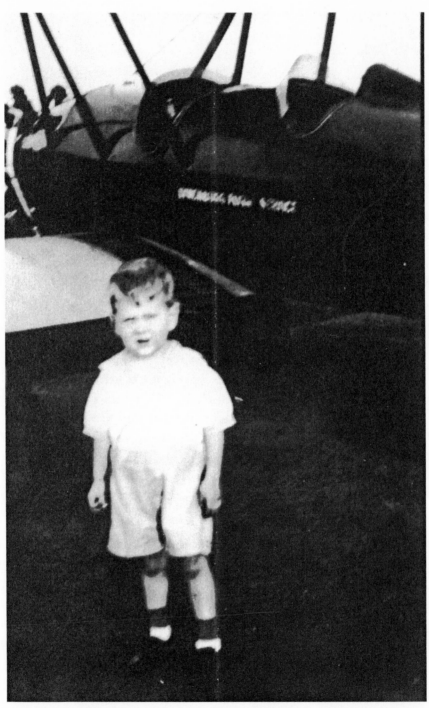

The author evincing a very early love of airplanes, c.1930

To most youngsters of that time and place, the Depression looked "normal" because that was all they had known for most of their lives. Donald had no basis for comparison and no reason or need to hope for something better. It takes a lot to make a kid unhappy, and this kid was not as bad off as many others. This he knew, but he had no genuine appreciation for his observation.

When he was born, Calvin Coolidge was president, but the very next year Herbert Hoover came into office. After the crash of '29, and for the next four years of Hoover's presidency, Donald heard frequent complaints about Hoover: how he had brought about the stock market crash and the poverty that followed and why destitute people had to live in "Hoovervilles," shacks made of scrap lumber and tin and thrown up around some cities. When Franklin Delano Roosevelt took office in 1933 and promised everybody a "New Deal," Donald could notice the immediate change in people's spirits.

He once saw President Roosevelt on the back platform of "The Roosevelt Special," his special campaign train, while the train was stopped in the station at Winder, Georgia, in 1933, not long before FDR's inauguration. Donald had just arrived by train in Winder with his mother to meet his grandfather for the car ride to Athens, where they would visit his grandparents and other relatives. Only days before "The Roosevelt Special" had stopped in Lynchburg at the foot of 9th Street. In both places, the assembled crowd was joyful, and some shouted "No more Depression!" They were wrong; there were six more years to come.

Streetcar heading up Fifth Street

CHAPTER 3

The Depression at Its Peak

꒰Donny began kindergarten during the school year 1933-34. The family had just moved from Rivermont Avenue to a single-family house at 170 Norfolk Avenue, only one long block away, on the other side of the Randolph-Macon Woman's College campus. He wasn't at all happy about attending kindergarten at Garland-Rodes School, another two blocks away on Rivermont Avenue, and made a scene the first time he was dropped off there.

In time he got used to the routine: games, stories, letter- and number-recognition—actually, he knew all that before because his mother had taught him while she cooked and he played with his blocks on the kitchen floor—and besides, he very much liked the pretty, young assistant teacher and piano player, "Miss Ruth" (Covington), as all the children called her. He didn't feel the same way about the kindergarten teacher herself, Miss Elizabeth Portner; she was old and bossy. (She must have been all of 50.) He was also bored with having to spread out a mat and take a nap every day. There were better things to do with one's time than sleep! Worst of all, twice a morning all the children had to line up for the toilets. Somebody always wet his or her pants and made a mess on the floor. Disgusting.

When parents arrived around noon, Donny was ready to get out of there.

The family lived on Norfolk Avenue only a couple of years. That end of the street was precipitous but wonderful for sledding in the winter. The police closed it to traffic sometimes for hours on end—even at night—so that the kids could go ripping down the middle of the street on their sleds. Occasionally, college girls from RMWC would bring their sleds and invite the children to hop on their backs and ride down the long, steep hill. It was really great fun. With all that added weight the sled would go like the wind. It was also kind of nice riding down the hill on a pretty girl's back or up front between her legs.

One day, while Donny was walking home from first or second grade—it is no longer quite clear—somebody rushed out of Butler's drugstore on the corner of Norfolk and Rivermont and told him his house was on fire. He hurried down the hill to his house, and sure enough, there were the firemen—nobody said "firefighters" in those days—with their beautiful trucks and hoses. They had put the fire out, but Donny's mother sadly pointed out the severe damage to the kitchen ceiling, which was falling in. The smell of burnt wood was everywhere, and much of the furniture in the living room and bedrooms had been damaged by both fire and water. The family had to take up residence in a hotel for several weeks while the workmen repaired the house. This house, like all of the family's houses up to this point, was rental property, and it was up to the landlord to arrange or approve everything. However, for lack of money, Donny's mother said, it was going to be next to impossible to replace several uninsured pieces of furniture and two closets of clothing.

At least Donny's family didn't have to move away permanently, as the family did next door. It was puzzling for a kid to witness. The people's furniture was suddenly one day unloaded onto the street. When he asked what had happened, his father said the people had been evicted because they couldn't pay their rent. Donald would not have known what the word "evicted" meant if he hadn't seen the word in action.

The family remained on Norfolk Avenue for about another year. Donald—and people were now beginning to call him by his full name, as his father always did—walked to and from school each day, a total distance of close to 1¼ miles, something unheard of for a kid today. It was good exercise, cost nothing, and was completely safe. There was admittedly a huge chow that lived on the way and would rush out to the sidewalk from behind the hedge around the house and bark fiercely at Donald as he walked by. Luckily, the dog never bit anybody.

It was rare to see an overweight kid in those days, let alone an obese one. The few who did manage to swell up were often taunted as "fatsos." Parents invariably told their children not to call others "fatsos," for "they probably have a glandular problem." One did wonder, for food was generally not that abundant in the middle 1930s.

It is true that in those days everybody ate bread and real butter—oleo, later called margarine, hadn't come on the market—bacon or sausage and eggs with biscuits made with pure lard for breakfast, and drank whole milk, pasteurized or raw, glass bottles of which were left on one's doorstep every day. In the winter the milk would freeze, and the cardboard tops would be lifted up several inches by the expansion. Cereal tasted especially good if you poured on it the rich cream at the top of the bottle. These items were readily available during the Depression and didn't cost all that much. Really good meat at 15-25 cents a pound for either of the other two meals was quite another matter. Sliced bacon could cost as much as 38 cents a pound. Coffee was close to 35 cents a pound. There was heavy reliance on canned goods at 8-10 cents for a no. 2 can; fresh fruits and vegetables in season were even less expensive. One dime would usually get you three pounds of apples.

Farmers had done especially well before and during World War I, but agriculture slumped during the 1920s and scarcely recovered throughout the 1930s. Distressed farmers agitated constantly for relief. Production dropped. Donald knew this, for his maternal grandfather and his mother's brother and brother-in-law were all farmers. Family conversation and letters dwelt on drought, boll weevils, and farmers who became tenants on their own land, which they had had to sell in order to survive. Those who couldn't find jobs picked fruits and vegetables for subsistence wages or all too often migrated from the farms to urban communities and essentially became vagrants begging for handouts. Some of these Donald saw "riding the rails" on passing freight trains and hanging out as hoboes at the city limits not far away at Princeton Circle. Others he saw standing in bread lines downtown.

The fortunate ones went into industry, especially the automotive industry up North, with output rising spectacularly throughout the 1920s and 1930s. However, nobody was concerned about being asphyxiated by bus or car fumes when taking a walk! First of all, there weren't any city buses; public transportation was by streetcar. Secondly, the number of cars on the road was pretty low by today's standards. The highways were almost all two-lane roads, and the side roads and many streets in many cities were unpaved. Flat tires were a constant nuisance.

When people did go riding in cars, which was often on Sunday afternoon, there were no seat belts or air bags. Because of narrow, curvy roads and cars with poor suspension, car sickness could be a problem, especially for people riding in the back seat. Donald had his share of wooziness—another good reason for learning to drive! And people stayed dressed up on Sunday. They couldn't shop because nothing was open, so they rode around or stayed home and received visitors. Being dressed up all day put a quietus on rough-housing.

During the week, if you were out walking somewhere and had a chance to hop in the back of a truck or in a rumble seat or on a running board, you did that gladly and without thought to your safety. Neither did anyone hesitate to thumb a ride. Thirdly, kids' parents then were not particularly protective. The idea that you could get "mugged" in those days—the word had not even been invented—never occurred to anyone. Moreover, if a kid's parents should act in an overprotective way, the kid suffered from the taunts of his playmates, who called him "a mama's boy."

Walking back from school alone one cold, snowy winter day Donald stopped just short of Norfolk Avenue and watched the motorman step out of his streetcar and lower the current collector, or power pole, at one end of the car and reposition it. Something must have seemed to be out of order, for the motorman normally lowered and raised the current collectors only at the end of the trolley line, preparatory to changing direction and heading back to town. In those days the end of the line was at Rivermont Park just beyond RMWC, another two blocks away. Donald had observed this operation many times in different places, but it always fascinated him. The motorman had to tug hard on the cable to pull the collector down level with the top of the car, and then he had to take up the cable slack on the spindle in front. He reversed this procedure at the other end of the car. When that pole was raised to come into contact with the overhead wire, there were always beautiful flashes of electricity and a loud crackling sound. (See the photo on page 14.)

Today it was different because the motorman's aim was bad, and he kept glancing the connector roller off the overhead wire and not seating it properly. Many more sparks than usual were created, and before anybody was aware, the top of the streetcar was on fire. Apparently, some leaves, stuck in the top channeling, had ignited. They began immediately to burn into the wood of the roof. Someone at The College Pharmacy on the corner must have called the fire department because those beautiful red engines appeared in a jiffy. The firemen put the blaze out in a few minutes. Most of the people aboard the streetcar had already gotten off, but the few who remained got off quickly when they became aware of the fire. Everybody just stood around and watched. Donald was absolutely gleeful to have a ringside seat! This time it wasn't his house burning down.

When the incident was over, Donald asked himself which he would rather be, a streetcar motorman or a fireman. It was a hard choice, so he settled for running all the way home and telling his mother about the wonderful event.

Aerial view of corner of Rivermont and Norfolk Avenues, showing portion of RMWC and block in which were located the College Pharmacy and Thornhill's Grocery

CHAPTER 4

The College Pharmacy and Thornhill's Grocery

ꝺ￫The College Pharmacy was located on the corner of Rivermont and Norfolk Avenues. Next to it was a beauty shop, where Donald's mother could get her hair done on rare occasions and read *Vogue* magazine for free, and next to that business was Thornhill's Grocery. There may even have been another shop in between. There was nothing startlingly unusual about the drugstore; the same can't be said for the grocery store. But, really, you needed to go inside both of them, look around, and meet the people.

This drugstore was typical of others in the 1930s. It had a long counter with stools that twirled round and round and were just a bit high for Donald. At that counter you could get a Coca-Cola—the name "Coke" had not yet been trademarked, yet you could order an "ammonia coke"—a delicious milkshake, or banana sundae for just 10—or was it 15 cents? (Hot fudge on your sundae cost an extra nickel.) The times being what they were, though, it was actually a rare occasion when Donald had 15 cents to spend that way. After all, his allowance had only recently been advanced to 25 cents a week.

As an aside, it should be noted that in those days segregation was in full effect, and Negroes—that was the proper polite designation then—were not welcome at tables or counters where food was served, although the store readily accepted their money for takeout and other items. Neither did they attend school with the whites but had their own separate public school system. Restaurants and toilets were also separate. On streetcars and buses the races were loosely separated with blacks at the rear. The prominently posted sign on streetcars, and later on buses, read: Whites to Front, Colored to Rear.

Across from the soda counter was the tobacco counter. Cigarettes cost only 10-15 cents a pack. Rolling your own was even cheaper. Men also chewed tobacco and smoked cigars and pipes and sometimes splurged on 10-cent El Productos and 15-cent cans of Half and Half pipe tobacco. Donald occasionally asked pipe smokers for their Half and Half cans; there were so many imaginative things you could do with a flat can with beveled sides that collapsed to half its size. The advantage to smokers was, of course, that the can took up only half the space in your pocket after you had finished half the tobacco. One day Donald bought two cigars for his father in the drugstore with a dollar bill that he remembers was bigger than the regular ones. His father called it a "floogie," or something like that. The bill size was reduced about this time to the present size, and the big bills soon began to disappear. Years later one surfaced in a drawer of a chest at home.

Past some skinny-legged little tables with skinny-legged, round-bottomed chairs scattered around the middle of the floor, at the far end of the store, was the pharmacy, where "Dr." Butler, as he was usually addressed, worked tirelessly day and night. Donald found it curious that people addressed a pharmacist by the title of "doctor," yet seldom extended that courtesy to dentists, chiropractors, podiatrists, or professors with doctoral degrees. In later years a pharmacist by the name of "Dr." Pearson established a drugstore one block east of Norfolk Avenue. He had three sons, one of whom, Nae Hugh, was Donald's age and two of whom were younger. Eventually, all three boys became pharmacists, and each inherited a drugstore from their father—the original, one at Peakland on Boonsboro Road, and one in Fort Hill.

It early became obvious to Donald that the Depression had not had an appreciable monetarily depressing effect on drugstores, and he briefly considered studying pharmacy rather than becoming a fireman or a motorman or an airline pilot. However, he soon concluded the job was too confining and boring. All day and half the night just standing behind a counter, reaching for bottles and mixing and pounding stuff—he wasn't that hungry. He had to confess: What he mainly liked about the drugstore was its daily use by youngsters as a gathering place, inside and out front, on their way to or from school.

Donald never spent a lot of time hanging out at the drugstore, as some kids did. But it was a place you could trade baseball cards and postage stamps or sell a possession for enough money to go to the movies, which could cost as little as a dime or 15 cents (age 12 and under) on Saturday at the Academy or the Isis (usually known as "The Armpit"), unless, of course, the Academy had a stage show, in which case it cost more.

One or two of the rich kids from farther out the Avenue or from what was then way out in Peakland had nifty bicycles he used to gaze at. Then there was, of course, the pharmacy's delivery motorcycle that was parked right on the corner. A genuine Harley-Davidson. Every now and then the colored delivery man would come out of the drugstore with several prescriptions. He would put them in one of the two saddle bags slung over the back fender and start the engine. What a roar! You stood as close as you dared while he jumped on the starter and revved the engine. He took off like a bolt down Norfolk Avenue or, with his left foot dragging the pavement, turned the thing around and headed up to Rivermont. Delivery was free. Good for business at the drugstore and welcomed by many customers who couldn't come to the store.

Thornhill's held an interest of quite a different sort. It was certainly not a gathering place for school kids but a place children in the neighborhood were introduced to early on when they went grocery shopping with one of their parents.

In those days grocery stores didn't look like grocery stores today—and bore no resemblance whatsoever to modern super-markets. Thornhill's was even less typical than most food stores of the 1930s. First of all, it was not part of a chain, as, for example, A & P or Piggly-Wiggly, but was privately owned and operated.

Secondly, it was old, and old looking, unlike other markets. Therein lay its charm for a kid like Donald.

Thornhill's had not suffered from the Depression as much as the chain stores because the management readily extended credit to customers residing nearby. Since this was one of the top neighborhoods of the city, most people living in the area could eventually pay their bills—certainly within 30 days. If the store had been located in one of the neighborhoods closer to the downtown area, it would have been a different story.

Having said all that, some pertinent observations are in order. Donald noticed that Thornhill's was not just old-fashioned, it was run-down. The screen in the door at the front was torn in several places and admitted flies galore. Since in those days there was no air conditioning, a screened door was a necessity, for the only other openings in the store were, to the best of my recollection, three windows high up on one side and one or two on the other side. A clerk opened and shut them with a 10-foot pole. The front windows on either side of the entrance, in which fruits and vegetables were stacked and large posters announcing specials inside were displayed, were of plate glass. It is a wonder that the produce on display didn't succumb to the summer sun streaming in. Well, as a matter of fact, that often happened, and the food was put on special at the end of the day.

For Donald, stepping inside Thornhill's Grocery was always an adventure in the making. For one thing, the place was dark and damp and, up front, smelled of produce; in the back, where the meat counter was located, the smell somehow reminded him of barns on his grandfather's farm. There were often live chickens in cages waiting to be killed and dressed for sale, squabs in smaller cages hung up high, and heads and heads of lettuce and cabbages in crates on the floor. From time to time a clerk would pull a chicken out of a cage and take it behind the meat counter preparatory to filling a customer's order. A few customers preferred that their chicken have its legs tied so that they could carry it home upside down and *au naturel,* as it were. It was cheaper than having the market kill and dress the chicken.

Donald used to watch hamburger in the making. The butcher would take gobs of red meat and run it through a hand-operated grinder bolted to one of the work tables just in front of the meat counter, close to the wall. The stringy product was caught in a bowl as it came out of the bottom of the grinder and the bowl placed in one of the refrigerated cases. This was certainly straightforward work, thought Donald.

The matter of sausage making was another story. In these times Donald had watched his mother add some diced potatoes or cereal or rice to hamburger to make it go farther, but until he witnessed sausage making at Thornhill's he did not know that this was done in stores before selling the product. It was an eye-opener.

One day he was watching the grinder in operation as a clerk fed pork chunks into it. As usual, the meat came oozing out the bottom, and the man caught it in a bowl and chopped it up fine. He then set the bowl over on the work table, reached across to the wall, and took down a dust scoop and a little broom. Leaning down, he swept up the floor under his work table, collecting scraps of meat, bits of sawdust, and goodness only knows what else, and dumped the whole shebang into the sausage bowl for mixing with salt, pepper, and spices before stuffing it in some membranous casing. With two fingers he carefully rescued a couple of pieces of lettuce or cabbage that had been dislodged from a crate and tossed them back on the floor. Was this a money-saving operation? Donald asked himself. Revolting! he thought. In addition to whatever the clerk had added to the ground sausage, there would be a lingering taste of oil in the mouths of unsuspecting consumers, for just before closing each night, the clerks mopped the floor with oil and then shook on some sawdust for drying. In the morning they swept up what they could.

Thornhill's had an elevator, a device never before or since seen by Donald in a grocery store. It was found just to the right of the main goods counter on the left of the store, past the produce but up from the meat counter. It was a freight elevator, completely open, with only a half-height gate that closed when the elevator began to move—in other words, somewhat similar to the *pater noster* encountered in Europe. The elevator was needed to bring up meat and produce from the basement below, where deliveries from jobbers had been received. There was a narrow driveway to the right of the store down which trucks backed for unloading. The driveway sloped steeply, so by the time it had reached the rear of the store, it was at basement, not first-floor, level. Donald once begged Mr. Thornhill himself to let him ride on the elevator. He went all the way to the bottom and back up again and stepped out with a smile on his face.

Donald could ask himself, if he thought of doing so—and he didn't—whether life was good and without a hint of the troubles occasioned by the Depression. His answer would have surely been, "Everything is hunky-dory." But the druggist and the grocer would not have agreed. Life consisted of very hard work, long hours, and not very much money.

CHAPTER 5

The Peak Tapers Off

𝔢❧In 1936 the family rented its second single-family home on a quiet side street not far from Garland-Rodes School. The house had three rooms downstairs—living room, dining room, and kitchen—and two bedrooms and a bath upstairs. The basement was dank and forbidding, and the attic storage space was accessible only with great difficulty.

The one telephone sat on a tiny table on a tiny stairway landing just three steps up from the living room. In those days relatively few households had telephone service, and of those that did, scarcely any had more than one instrument. Because he was away on business three weeks out of four, Donald's father felt he ought to have one installed at home.

The phone consisted of a heavy, round base with a tall pedestal, which served as a handle when holding the phone, at the top of which was the mouthpiece. A separate earpiece hung on a hook attached to the pedestal. It wasn't until the 1940s that cradle-type phones became readily available. All were black. Colors came later yet. Telephones were considered to be mainly a means of rapid and brief business communication—not that people didn't chat on them locally. Long-distance calls were a rarity because of the expense.

In the beginning there was no dialing; you just told the operator what number you wanted, and she connected you. Numbers in small towns were, by today's standards, incredibly short: for example, 4528 or 633 or 89 or even just a single number! In a few

27

Odessa, the author, and his mother at 208 Ash Street

tiny communities, all you had to do was ask for the person you wanted to talk to. Donald remembers that at his maternal grandparents' house in Athens, Georgia, he had only to turn a crank twice to ring his aunt and uncle on the farm and three times to get them at their house in town. Two longs and one short ring would rouse somebody at the sawmill. Of course, everybody connected to the country line would hear the various rings. You were only supposed to pick up on your ring, but there were times when curiosity prompted somebody to listen in on your conversation. Donald's grandmother was a past master at noticing the drop in volume, which usually signaled the presence of an uninvited party. She didn't hesitate to communicate her displeasure to the eavesdropper.

In time, a few telephone numbers had letters added: for example, 305-J. When dialing came about, and the numbers in large cities necessarily became longer, prefixes based on familiar regional names were used to form exchanges: for examples, AD (for Adams) 2-4828. When you received a long-distance call—always bad news—the operator, often known as "Central," invariably announced: "Long distance calling." Donald was at home each time when calls announcing the death of one of his grandfathers and one of his grandmothers came through. His paternal grandfather had died in 1933, before they had telephone service, so the family in South Carolina had to send a telegram. He remembers the knock on the door of the Rivermont Avenue apartment that day when a uniformed young man delivered the yellow and black Western Union envelope with the bad news.

Across the front of the house at 208 Ash Street was a long porch on which people actually sat and talked. Off the kitchen was a stoop, where we put the garbage can and left dirty garden shoes. The front yard was small, but the back yard was fairly deep. The property was not very wide, perhaps 50 feet, a typical width for lots in town. Donald's father said the rent was high—$35 a month.

There were two other boys in the neighborhood and one girl. Billy Osborn, who lived next door, seemed to have everything a

Billy, Odessa, the author, and homemade airplane in back yard

boy could wish for: plenty of cars, trucks, trains, play guns, and a complete cowboy outfit. But he wore glasses, was uncoordinated, and couldn't pitch or catch a ball. His father was a watchmaker for Buckingham and Flippin downtown who owned not one, but two Packards, a luxury much out of keeping with the times. He barely tolerated his son's awkwardness and settled for pitching baseballs to Donald—very hard, in fact. But Donald caught them all even though his gloved hand often turned red. Billy picked his nose a lot and screamed and cried like a baby when he didn't get his way. Donald never understood him, but they used to play cowboys together on stick horses in Billy's back yard where, at the far end, they had built what they called "the barracks," out of tree branches, from which they could shoot Indians and bad white men. Very low-budget entertainment to fit the times. Our heroes were Buck Jones, Gene Autry, Tom Mix, and Hopalong Cassidy.

In retrospect, these legendary cowboys were always in the right, filled with courage and honesty, of impeccable morals, and well-mannered—particularly toward women. They never lost a fist fight or a gun battle and, though sometimes they incurred a "flesh wound," they never died. They drove home the point that right was right and wrong was wrong. A powerful message for youngsters.

The other boy, John East, was obese and lived just three doors away at the end of Ash Street, on Columbia Avenue. He spent a lot of his time blowing his trumpet on his front porch. His family did not own even one car. One day a steel-guitar salesman conned John's mother into buying her son an instrument and six months of lessons at a price the family could not afford during these hard times. Donald can still hear John's father yelling at his wife for having jeopardized their financial security with "such frivolity." For his part, John simply alternated between blowing his trumpet and playing his steel guitar on the front porch, to the annoyance of the neighbors. He had a particularly bad habit of practicing early in the morning, well before breakfast. He couldn't play either instrument worth a darn.

The girl, Odessa, was just Donald's age—and cute. In fact, she seemed sort of exotic because she had a French last name, Pregeant, and her father was a Knight Templar (of the Masons), who had a beautiful, long sword that he wore with his dress uniform of some then unknown sort. They had come from the big city of Richmond, another thing that set them apart from everybody else.

Actually, there was one other girl nearby, a Jewish girl, Ruth Berman, whose parents owned Snyder & Berman, a dry goods store in town. She lived in a bigger and better brick house than anybody else's up on the avenue on the corner and did not normally associate with the kids down the block. Her house had a stone lion on each side of the front entrance. The boys didn't exactly think she was snooty, but she did seem to have much more money than anybody else.

Of all the children in the neighborhood, Donald was the only one with a pet, first a white cat named Snowball and then, upon the cat's disappearance after two years, a dog named Scrappy. When Donald asked several of his friends why they too didn't have a pet, they usually answered that their parents said it was just too expensive to feed one. But Donald never quite believed that story because he knew that cats could feed themselves very well by catching mice and dogs would eat mostly scraps from the table, with an occasional can of commercial dog food. Actually, it may well have been true that some people could not afford a pet.

Donald's family had a nice upright, cabinet-style radio in a corner of the living room to the left of the front door. It must have cost at least $60! Donald spent several hours each week listening to his favorite programs, such as "The Green Hornet," "Amos 'n' Andy," "Lum and Abner," "The Shadow," "The Lone Ranger," plus others. No program was censored by parents in those days. There was no need to guard the children against profanity, obscenity, irreligiosity, or even relativism; such did not come across the airways.

Few people had victrolas, an old word for record player, so there was no readily available music with questionable lyrics. The local

station played records, of course—mostly ballads—and sometimes the needle would get stuck in a groove. Listeners would
frequently yell out loud to "Mush Mouth"—that's what they
called the announcer—that the record was stuck, and although
it was certain the announcer downtown couldn't hear those goofy
people, he did move the needle back in place when he returned
from the toilet, or wherever, but with a loud, scratching sound.
Everybody's flesh would crawl.

Until the 1940s all records were made of bakelite and shel-
lacked. They were very subject to warping and scratching, and if
the turntable was not absolutely level, the needle would skitter
across the surface, producing dreadful sounds as well as damage.
Skipping was also a problem with the 33s and 45s that followed
the 78s because the grooves were narrower, making a precisely
level surface imperative. Speakers were, for the most part, only
adequate; there were no woofers and tweeters and big, booming
bass boxes. And as for portable radios, it was a long time before
their appearance. Nice to take on an outing, it was nevertheless
like carrying another picnic basket. Furthermore, few people
could afford them.

There was, of course, no television in those days. Donald saw
his first telecast in 1937 or 1938 at a demonstration downtown
at the Virginian Hotel. He stood inside a curtained booth not
unlike a voting booth and witnessed on a screen in black and
white a female singer rendering "Red Sails in the Sunset" to
the accompaniment of a small band about 40 feet away in the
lobby. It was another 10 years before the family acquired its own
set. People then would watch anything, no matter how bad the
program—even a test pattern.

The refrigerator, a GE Turret Top, surmounted by a cooling coil
with fins, was small but adequate for the family's needs. Besides,
plenty of people did not have a refrigerator as such—after all,
most cost around $100—just an ice box, like the one Donald's
family had when they first moved to town. It was just a wooden
chest with a compartment for ice on top. In South Carolina and

Aerial photo of Preston Glenn Airport

Georgia, Donald's grandparents also maintained, in addition to an icebox, a "safe," a kind of transitional non-refrigerated latticed cabinet where the food from a meal was stored if it was going to be used at another meal that day. You certainly didn't throw any food away. Donald quickly learned that biscuits were perpetually available from the safe.

But back to the house on Ash Street and to Donald's room. It was ideally constructed for his needs, with a dormer nook in the front part and two windows on the side. With the help of his father, Donald constructed a model train table under the window in the dormer recess. It was a fairly large table extending almost all the way back to his bed, with a cut-out in the middle so that he could get to his tracks and wiring more easily.

In those days there were only full-size model trains: standard, O- and O-27 gauges, no HO- or N-gauge. To have a decent model railroad, a rather large space was required. Donald had to make do for his O-gauge equipment with the space he had. Train engines and cars were expensive—some cars cost as much as a dollar apiece. They made ideal birthday and Christmas gifts, and Donald looked forward each year to adding one or two cars to his fleet. The O-gauge and O-27 tracks and equipment were essentially the same and somewhat smaller than the standard size. Once in a while Donald augmented his collection by looking around at second-hand sales; he also traded with other boys and thus varied his running stock. Model train layouts were high on the list of boys' hobbies back then.

So was model airplane construction. Kits for rubber band-powered models could be obtained for as little as 10 or 25 cents. Hardly anyone could afford a gas-powered kit and little engine. Besides, if you had the money to build and fly one, you would worry constantly that it would crash and you'd lose your entire investment. Not that the rubber band-powered versions didn't crash. Oh, they did all right, but somehow a boy could always make repairs and get the thing flying again. Once in a while, Donald would even set fire to one of his oldest planes and let it burn and

Preston Glenn Airport

crash at will just like a military plane being shot down. Or, like so many others, he was reminded of Amelia Earhart when she presumably crashed after disappearing in 1937. He made frequent trips to the airport, where he saw some of the early multi-passenger airplanes, including the famous Ford Trimotor, which whetted his appetite for flying.

The most complete line of model planes was available downtown at Bragassa's, a wonderful store on 12th Street that featured not only various hobby items but also guns, knives, and ammo, as did Fisher's Sporting Goods on lower Main. In those days boys were encouraged by their fathers to do "boy" or "men" things: building or repairing, shooting, hunting. Inculcated within all kids, though, was a big sense of responsibility. Sayings abounded: Treat every gun as if loaded. Never point a gun at anybody or anything you do not intend to shoot. Sharpen your knives but keep them sheathed. A penknife is for cleaning fingernails; a 6-inch blade is a weapon. Treat it as such. Remember that even a .22 bullet is dangerous within one mile. On the range keep your guns pointed down-range. Keep your dog in view as you raise your shotgun to fire at birds, otherwise you'll have a dead dog for supper.

Donald set up an old card table under one of the side windows in his room when he was about to begin building a balsa wood airplane. He could lay out and thumb-tack plans to the surface and not worry about the holes he was making. It was the same with the many pins he used to secure the pieces of each phase of the wooden frame of the plane as the glue dried. And when he applied dope to the tissue paper covering, it didn't matter if the drips got on the table. His mother probably found all this construction an eyesore, but she never said anything. After all, it took days to build such an airplane, and the endeavor kept Donald out of mischief. All this entertainment for only one dollar or less! Model trains, planes, and books—educationally valuable, hands-on activities calculated to produce later technical experts and engineers, aviators, thinkers, and scholars, and all in keeping with the Depression—for a pittance.

It is common wisdom that the Depression lasted about 10 years and that it peaked during 1932-34—that is to say, the worst economic conditions obtained during that mid period. For some people, the hardship began and extended considerably longer. Most families noticed little change in the cost of staple foods—bread a dime a loaf and milk a dime a quart, beans and rice a few cents a pound, homegrown fruits and fresh vegetables not much more, meat 25-50 cents a pound, chicken and fish less.

New automobiles—Fords, Chevys, and Plymouths mostly—stayed steady at about $500-600. To people of the 21st century, this price is unbelievably low, but to a family in the 1930s it was anything but cheap. The average price of a new house actually dropped during the Depression from around $5000 to close to $4000 in the mid '30s and then went back up to $5000+ by 1940. Those hurting the most were people without permanent employment, on relief, often ill, short on clothes and shoes, with children to feed, without insurance or health care, living in public housing or other low-rent property—people filled with discouragement, barely making it day by day.

That the peak was actually tapering off by 1935-36 is easier to say in retrospect than to remember, but for a kid growing up then it meant perhaps more ice cream cones or even a new bicycle. Somehow, slowly but surely, frugality became an essential part of living. This forced virtue became, for Donald and his friends, a fact of life never to be forgotten.

CHAPTER 6

Knickers, BB Guns,
and the Johnson Smith Catalog

ल This chapter is part of the sequence of chapters and events that precede. It also reaches forward a couple of years beyond the last chapter. Its purpose is to catalog impressions and activities that were ongoing during the decade 1928-1938.

Younger readers or listeners will probably not know what knickers are, and neither will they know that the word is a shortened form of knickerbockers. Most certainly they will not know this item of clothing was named after Diedrich Knickerbocker, the fictitious Dutch author of Washington Irving's *History of New York* (1809).

But what are knickers? They are short, rather loose trousers gathered in just below the knees and resemble those worn by the Dutch settlers of New York, or, as it was called then, New Amsterdam. Probably most often the fabric was corduroy. In some ways, they remind one of the baggy, lightweight pants, but closefitting at the ankles, worn by women. However, unlike harem pants, there is nothing sexy about knickers. At least not to men and boys.

And therein, I wager, lay part of the distaste that boys of the Depression era had for this piece of apparel. As a rule, boys were not—*are* not?—enamored of displaying their bare legs in public. Besides, in the winter it was downright cold with all that leg exposed—unless, of course, you also wore long socks, which were common. Even the girls, who presumably had no aversion to displaying their legs, froze in the winter in their dresses and socks. But there was no such thing as slacks for either sex.

In many ways long socks were an undesirable sartorial accoutrement: They kept falling down, particularly while running somewhere at breakneck speed. Donald's mother had a solution: Wrap rubber bands inside the folded-down socks and over the sleeve of the knickers. Only trouble was the tight, narrow rubber bands cut off circulation and left scary-looking red blood bands around the top of the lower legs. Not a good idea. Quick reversion to short socks and cold—later—hairy legs. Donald knew a few kids who wore no socks. They all came from "the other side of town," as people were accustomed to saying. It wasn't the style; they simply didn't have the money to buy socks.

Boys wanted to wear long pants, but it was not allowed until they were adolescents. (This is the old-fashioned word for "teenagers" in case younger readers/listeners don't know!) Not even to church. Knickers were worn to school with open-necked shirts, to church with a tie and jacket. As you walked, corduroy knickers scraped together with a distinctive whop-whop sound. Most knickers had elastic sleeves just below the knees, but a few were secured by a band with a button or little buckle. To remove knickers, you had to take off your shoes. If you pulled the knickers off over your shoes, you worsened the problem of slippage because you would invariably over-stretch the elastic sleeves. Then the knickers wouldn't stay up at all. But, no matter their condition, nobody poked fun because all boys had to wear these things. Donald's parents reminded him that boys in Europe had to wear them, too, but this was no consolation.

During warm weather boys got to wear shorts, although some mightily resisted because of their aversion to showing too much leg! Trouble was, there wasn't anything else to wear. Of course, lots of the country kids from Bedford and Campbell Counties wore overalls.

No one was ever able to explain why there was no resistance to donning bathing trunks at the pool, pond, ocean, or river. But children are not known for their reasonableness and consistency. One of Donald's close friends, Herb Harris, who was close to six feet by age 14, got to wear shorts all year round, even though there was constantly the risk that some boy would rush up and yank them down, exposing the unwitting victim's underwear. For a while he wore long socks when the weather was cold but soon gave up when he discovered they wouldn't stay up during the strenuous activities self-assigned by boys his age. So he gave up thereafter and just let his thick socks droop and drop. Not a pretty sight. He went all through high school like that, maybe because somebody had told him British boys dressed like that.

Styles have always changed from time to time, but out of financial necessity they didn't change much during the 1930s. Few people had the money to purchase fashionable, trendy clothes. It was as if people had settled on a uniform of the day: for boys, knickers and shorts; for girls, frocks; for men, baggy, overlong, generally uncreased pants; for women, housedresses. Hats and caps were worn by both sexes. Repairs to clothes were constantly being made. And people wore their "best" clothes to church. Overalls and such were for misfortunate farmers and hoboes and never constituted a "statement." A woman in public would not have been caught dead in work attire or ripped-up dungarees, let alone short shorts.

Boys loved guns of all kinds and were encouraged by their fathers to shoot and hunt. The first gun that boys acquired was a BB gun, usually a rifle, though occasionally a pistol, weapons that shot tiny, round pellets. These were cocked by a lever that compressed a spring. The rifle magazine held 100 or more—a whole cylindrical package—of BBs. Since a package cost only a nickel, a boy could shoot a lot for practically nothing. He would shoot paper targets, light kitchen matches stuck in the bark of trees, knock down bottles, and aim at fish in a pond and birds in trees. Deflection in the water sometimes saved the lives of the fish, but birds didn't fare quite so well, even though the accuracy of a BB gun is not all that great. Fathers always admonished their sons not to shoot at people, even in fun. One boy forgot and, while aiming low, nevertheless put out the eye of a friend. Real guns—.22's—came later, and the admonishments to be careful were turned up very high. Animals didn't fare as well as when the boys had only BB guns.

BB guns were usually Christmas presents, but the ammo could be purchased for a small portion of the boy's allowance or money earned by work. On the other hand, bullets for a .22 rifle cost much more, but few boys younger than 12 had a .22 rifle. In those days they were almost always single-shot rifles, a natural inhibitor to over-expenditure and overuse!

Back then all children were enjoined to save money, either by being mindful of the family's possessions and taking care of them so they would not have to be replaced soon or by always saving some of their allowance, their money earned by work, and their Christmas and birthday money. In addition, they usually had on their dresser a piggy bank, a little brass bank building, or some such depository for spare pennies and nickels, two denominations that actually had some purchasing power in those days. Every child could count on his mother to drop her spare change in a cookie jar in the kitchen. Mutual role models, in other words. When a child reached ten or so and began to work around the neighborhood, he (or she) was expected to open a savings account at the bank, if only a Christmas Club account. Frugality was a serious watchword.

If a boy read comic books—and what boy didn't?—they only cost a nickel or a dime—he couldn't miss the prominent Johnson Smith Company ad on the back cover. For one lousy 3-cent stamp he could get a three-inch-thick Johnson Smith catalog full of the most remarkable things this world has ever dreamed of: books of every description; magic tricks; a whoopee cushion—you slip it in somebody's chair, he sits on it, and a loud fart-like sound comes forth; a joy buzzer—you shake hands with somebody while holding the device, and it buzzes and tingles like the dickens; stuffed barking dogs; disgusting bug ice cubes; a snake-in-a-can that comes flying out the minute you open the can; a Jew's harp that will set your teeth on edge; itching powder (made of hair probably taken from a barber shop). All this stuff and Comet and Megow model airplane kits and much more would fascinate boys of all ages throughout the year. And you could order any of it simply by putting your coins in an envelope and mailing it off. Every day was an eternity until the package arrived.

Johnson Smith & Co.
Novelty Catalog from 1938

One day Donald found in somebody's trash can a wonderful object, a crystal radio complete with rheostatic volume control. It only lacked a cat's whisker to attach to the feeler arm in order to locate and draw in a radio station. Of course, Johnson Smith had cat's whiskers for next to nothing. Within a week Donald's junked radio was operating, with the antenna he strung out of one of his bedroom windows. Later, he did the job really right and constructed a transversal antenna in the attic and was able to pull in stations as far away as 50 miles. Total cost: 5 cents for the cat's whisker, 3 cents for postage, and 12 cents for antenna wire and two glass insulators. Real Depression living!

This was the radio Donald was listening to on Sunday night, October 30, 1938, when a musical program was cut off by a startling announcement of an invasion by Martians. He ran downstairs and tuned in the big Philco and told his parents what he had heard. They scoffed at the idea, but as bulletins kept coming in, they began to wonder whether it was for real. Of course, it wasn't true; there weren't any Martians; it was an incredibly realistic radio dramatization by Orson Welles of H. G. Wells's *The War of the Worlds* on the CBS drama series "The Mercury Theatre of the

Air." Radio, like TV years later, had assumed awesome power on that fateful night.

Elsewhere in the world even more awesome things were happening that would portend another world war. A Martian landing might well have been preferable.

CHAPTER 7

Elementary School

❧Donald entered first grade with a collection of children he had known from kindergarten and from his neighborhood. All were from middle class homes and had been only minimally deprived because of the Depression. These children's exposure to real want had been random and sporadic, and their lot had been improving in the last year or so. Few had any genuine abundance of clothes, food, or money, but no one was suffering.

Of Donald's friends only a couple entered private school; in those days almost everybody attended the public schools. Provided by tax monies, it was, of course, much cheaper than paying tuition and room and board away from home. But there was also a decent education to be had in the public school system—a standard sequence of courses in English, spelling, hand writing, history, mathematics, and science plus, later on, a number of electives.

Everybody took the same array of studies, regardless of economic or social background, which put competition on a more or less pure basis of achievement within each and every area. Allowances were not made for a normally slower start for boys or for girls' presumed inherent inability to achieve comparably in math and science. It was a simple, though certainly not perfect, system. Everybody was expected to do his or her very best. Those who didn't caught it first at school and then at home. This arrangement encouraged pupils to do their best all right, but it also prompted clever measures to insure academic success. And there is no group more inventive

Postcard of Garland-Rodes School

than pupils or students! (Like the Europeans, American speakers of English formerly made a distinction between pupils—children learning in the lower grades—and students—young people studying at the high school or higher level.)

Donald no longer remembers his first day at school, only that his teacher, Miss Mary Lou Tucker, was "sweet." (In those days kindergarten was not considered "school" as such, and there was no such thing as "pre-school" or "pre-kindergarten.") It must not have contained too much trauma, else he would have! He does remember the several classrooms at Garland-Rodes School; their main characteristic was roominess. There was always a wall of windows. In addition, there were blackboards on the remaining three sides. And the word was "blackboard," not chalkboard. And the color was black slate, not green.

There were teachers in all grades remembered—mostly affectionately—by former pupils for being the brunt of mischief or for transmitting relatively useless knowledge or opinions that nevertheless were retained for decades on end. For example, there was the bad boy (not I!) who put a large thumbtack in Mrs. Varn's chair. When she sat down, she leaped up immediately, searched her rear, pulled out the tack, and launched an investigation. Of course, nobody knew anything. From that time forth, Mrs. Varn never failed to brush out her chair before taking a seat.

Then there was Mrs. Rosa Ould's peculiar instruction to all that they should say "simultaneous" (with a short vowel in the first syllable as in the word "similar") and that they should always sing "righteously" as if it were spelled "righkiously." The rationale for the first pronunciation was that it was the latest; for the second, that is was "easier." Funny how such trivia sticks in the mind.

The girls and the boys had separate entrances, one at either end of the building. At recess they played in their respective playgrounds, where there were swings, acting bars, and a seesaw. You could even fly a kite you had made in or out of school out of newspaper, sticks or slim branches, glue, and string. By the way, no one thought it odd, let alone unlawful, to keep the sexes apart.

At indoor recess in the basement there was a line between the girls and the boys, and no one dared to cross it.

During fire drills, which were held unexpectedly about every month, girls and boys marched out and back in together but in closely regimented fashion. The activity would begin with the sound of a clanging brass bell high up on the hall wall rung personally by Miss Lizzie Harvey, the dour principal. The children would all line up in the classroom according to an agreed-upon arrangement and, severely admonished by the teacher not to talk, would proceed out of the building. They had earlier been instructed not to look around but to halt when ordered and to turn around only upon having received the order to do so, namely, shortly before returning to the building. (Presumably, if the building had really been on fire, seeing the conflagration would have caused some of the children "to go all to pieces." Donald felt he could speak for all the children present in expressing his fervent hope that the school was in flames and headed for total destruction so that all the children would have months off.) Having survived the drill, the children were in high spirits as they re-entered the school building, and some dared to talk. If any chatterboxes passed by Miss Harvey on the way back to class, she would literally snatch them out of line and lecture them on the serious nature of the exercise. She was such a fearsome woman that they were immediately squelched.

Everybody looked forward to recess, where much ripping and snorting took place. Everybody tried to do everything every time: swing on the acting bars, swing on the swings, climb the flagpole, and horse around on the seesaw. In the case of that last-named device, it was great fun to seesaw up and down a few times and, when you were in the down position, suddenly to get off the thing. That of course caused the person who was up very high to come crashing down to the ground. Many a fight began that way. A teacher would usually come over and break it up, but there was always time to get in a few good licks.

Recess was over when Otha the janitor came to the entrance door and rang a hand bell. Anybody who didn't scurry along would be castigated by the scowling principal, who seemed to be omnipresent, especially when you were up to something unauthorized.

Shenanigans in the classroom were handled by the teacher. That is, if she spotted them; and Donald was sure all teachers had eyes in the back of their head. Of course, the boys were almost invariably the instigators of mischief, and usually it was the boys who also bore the brunt of that mischief.

Tripping somebody was great fun. Since Donald had been tripped up by some of his friends, he enthusiastically reciprocated when he had the chance. Here is the scene. Desks were units consisting of a seat attached to the front of the desk behind and screwed to the floor. There were rows of desks from the front to the back of the room, with very little aisle space in between. This meant that a boy could unobtrusively stick his leg out and trip up someone walking down between the desks. It happened all the time, and the person tripped up went careening forward until he either stumbled and fell on the floor with a crash or somehow was able to arrest his fall at the last moment by grabbing onto someone's desk or arm, an act likely also to cause consternation. The boys never tripped girls, and girls never tripped anybody. This was a boy thing, and the teacher knew it. When someone went plunging to the floor, she—all teachers at this level were women—knew right away that a boy had caused the ruckus.

Despite the segregation of the sexes at the beginning of school and at recess, they were together in the classroom. Often they were seated alternately, from front to back. This meant that a boy often had a girl in front of him. A perfect arrangement!

Here is the explanation.

These old-fashioned desks were made to order for mischief. The surface of the desk contained a long groove that ran across the top. You put your pen and pencil in the groove to keep them from sliding or rolling down the desk top and onto the floor. To the right of the groove was an inkwell, that is, a cutout in the desk top into which a small bottle of ink was set. To write, you took the top off the ink bottle and dipped the steel-tipped pen.

To learn to write with a pointed pen required constant dipping and took both instruction and practice. The most popular system of writing at the time was the Locker system, which required endless drills—on the blackboard too—conducted by the teacher in a rhythmic, singsong fashion: round and round and round (drawing circles) or up down up down up down/push-pull, push-pull (making upward strokes). The pupils hated this part of each day. Most of them had great trouble in making these configurations on paper with a steel pen, and mothers were not happy about the ink splatters on white shirts and crisp frocks. You would think the process would produce some of the worst handwriting in the world. On the contrary, the kids learned cursive writing, not just printing (as has been the custom over the last 30 years), and maintained their skill over a lifetime. And phonics taught them to spell flawlessly.

But back to the inkwell, the source of so much pleasure for the boys. Some of the more seductive girls would lean far back in their seats and dangle their hair in the face of the boy seated behind them or rest their heads briefly on the boy's desktop. Instead of getting the message of "seduction underway"—after all, these were mostly 10-year-olds or thereabout—the boys seized the chance to pull a girl's hair or, worse yet, to dip the ends in their inkwell. Mild pandemonium would always ensue, and the teacher would come down the aisle to ascertain the cause of the racket. When the girl would accuse the boy of having dipped her curls in ink, the boy would simply look perplexed and tell the teacher he couldn't help it if the girl leaned way back and got her hair in the ink. The teacher would lecture both parties, and then the incident would be forgotten until the next time. If the boy was caught, he would be ordered to go stand in the cloak room.

The seats were hinged and had to be raised in order to exit from the desk unit. This meant that anybody behind who had his or her feet propped up on the exposed portion of the seat suffered mightily if the person in front suddenly returned to his desk and sat down heavily. At least a loud yell resulted, but more often than not the injured boy would haul off and slug the other guy. If it was a girl's feet that got pinched, she would start crying, which would also get a reaction out of the teacher. Nothing ever came of such incidents, though, because everybody claimed innocence.

Sometimes the guy in back would purposely press very hard on the surface of the upturned seat and prevent the fellow in front from sitting down. That always got a response from the teacher, but the standee was usually the castigated one, not the instigator.

Then there was the matter of shoe theft. The girls would often slip partially or entirely out of their shoes while at their desks. The boy behind would spot this activity and, with his outstretched foot, pull the girl's shoes under his desk. In a short while, either because she had to get up and go to the blackboard or simply began looking for her shoes, she would feel around with her feet but fail to find them. By then the culprit had probably kicked them clear out of their row so that some other mischief maker could hand on each shoe to other co-conspirators. Enter the teacher with her question why Mary Sweeney or Lois Scott or Martha Evans had come to school in sock feet or barefooted. Punishment was always threatened but seldom carried out for the simple reason that no one knew anything. The game took on a more serious note one day when a boy flung a girl's shoes out of the open window. In those days, there were no screens to prevent this sort of thing. It was not unheard of for books to go flying out as well.

Despite the occasional horseplay, a lot of learning took place. When grades were sent home after each six-week period, parents scrutinized them and rewarded or punished their children accordingly. Seldom did they rail against the teachers when the pupils did not perform optimally or were caught in mischievous acts. The assumption was that the pupils were at fault, not the teachers.

During these early school years friendships were begun and fashioned of sturdy stuff. Most of this group stayed together through all the years of public education. Male friendships were cemented, and interest in girls increased each year.

Children were constantly being admonished to remember that these were hard times and that they needed an education in order to succeed. They were told that those who didn't study hard and make good grades were likely to end up doing menial work the rest of their lives or joining the hoboes down at the railroad station. Those who worked hard in school could expect to become hall or room monitors or be allowed to dust erasers out on the front steps in the fresh air before the end of the day. They could then look forward to graduating from high school and, with a scholarship in hand, perhaps even go to college. And, one day much later, they might just become doctors, lawyers, bankers, or even motormen on the longest streetcar line!

CHAPTER 8

Junior High

ʔ꣸Junior high school back then was like junior high school or the end of middle school now, neither fish nor fowl. The boys and girls were neither pupils nor students, that is, they were not clearly defined as children or youth. Nor was their academic status as regards curriculum unequivocal. In other words, there was overlap in maturity and studies. Some appeared older than others, and reflected this growth in their study habits. Some retained a childishness of physiognomy and intellect. There was, of course, some overlapping that produced really smart, well-motivated baby-faced kids as well as a group of completely unmotivated brutes. Quite a mix.

In addition, the picture was complicated by the expectation that few of these pupils/students would ever attend college; in fact, it was assumed that not nearly all would even graduate from high school. A number went to work in one of the few local factories; some got a job driving a city bus after the streetcar tracks were paved over. This was the time that the law permitted youngsters to quit school without legal penalty, particularly after having finished the 8th grade. Junior high school now includes usually grades 7-9; middle school, 5-8. There was no middle school in the 1930s but only junior high school, which did in fact encompass part of grade 7 (so-called high-7) or 8 (low-8) and go through high-8. This arrangement was essentially caused by an 11-year school system establishing three years of senior high school.

The first thing that will strike the reader is that junior high school was, and is, the smallest, and least defined, block of study

Robert E. Lee Junior High School

years of all. Smaller than grammar school and high school, it is sandwiched between them, falling victim to the academic expectations on either side. This is one of the main reasons for its virtual disappearance in today's American school systems. Another reason is that a grammar/middle/high school arrangement accords better with the natural physical and psychological development of children. In grammar school the pupils are clearly children; in middle school, adolescents reaching puberty; in high school, youth or young adults.

In Lynchburg another factor was at play at Robert E. Lee Junior High: It drew its students from various parts of the city, producing a social mix not encountered at any of the elementary schools, some of which would be considered "elite," others "working class." In a small Southern city in those days the demarcation of social classes was significant, and not just because of segregation in those days, unlike today where the promotion of a "classless" society is the theoretical but impossible goal of many reformers. Nowadays, political correctness promotes the notion of equality of people in all respects, an unrealistic expectation where education is concerned. Even though more and more people may be attending, even graduating from college, those whose intellectual capabilities are not up to the task tend to lower the standards for everybody. In the 1930s, the opposite was true: If a student couldn't make the grade, he flunked out; remedial work was unheard of.

It was into this scene that college-oriented Donald stepped, together with many of his friends from grammar school. They encountered some of the same kind of students from the other side of town, but they also ran into students whose goals were completely undefined and who were largely troublemakers. School for the latter was a holding pattern, a way station between an elementary education and work.

Donald's and his friends' initial collision with an unfamiliar social class took place on the very first bus ride to school. Heretofore, Donald walked to his neighborhood school; now he had a 35-minute ride across town on a city bus. There were no school buses set aside for transporting students to and from their school, as most communities nowadays provide. Instead, one purchased reduced-rate student tokens at 7 cents each (four for a quarter), with free transfers, or a weekly pass for one dollar. To have a weekly pass was a status symbol, and students possessing one proudly displayed it. By this time, almost all of the streetcars had been replaced by buses, and gradually the streetcar tracks were blacktopped over.

Everything proceeded normally for the first half of the ride across town until the bus stopped to pick up some kids from the oldest part of the city. It is impossible to remember who started the ruckus, but words like "trash" and "conceited"—both favorite accusatory words in those days—were tossed back and forth until two boys got into a real fist fight right in the aisle. It got so bad that the driver pulled up the brake, left his seat, and came back to break up the fight.

There were other bus rides of which Donald was not proud. The war effort required that people save their scrap metal and turn it in to designated collection points. The two high schools—one white, one colored—and the junior high were among the major places collecting donated metal ranging from tools to tire irons, hub caps, engine parts, sheet metal strips, and maybe even anvils. One bus route to the junior high led up 12th Street, just off which was located Dunbar, the colored high school. On numerous oc-casions the Negro students would be carrying pieces of metal as they walked to their school; the white students were holding theirs on their lap on the bus as they passed by.

One day somebody let loose with a racial epithet—Donald is no longer certain which group it came from—and the barrage began. Colored students hurled pieces of scrap metal at the bus while the white students flung theirs out of the windows. An altogether disgraceful occurrence that caused the bus driver to stop his bus and intervene. No doubt, the matter was reported at both schools, but Donald does not remember the outcome.

Classes at the junior high were, by and large, serious business. The teachers tried very hard to teach, and most of the students were interested in learning, even if some of them were fonder of shop, metal working, and gym than academic subjects. The Depression was winding down somewhat, but jobs were not all that plentiful except in the Works Projects (earlier Progress) Administration (WPA), which had received additional federal money in 1938 to sponsor many public projects, and the Civilian Conservation Corps (CCC), a government organization that concentrated on planting trees. The sharpest academic memory Donald has for this level of school was the required reading of John Steinbeck's classic Dust Bowl novel *The Grapes of Wrath*, the unforgettable story of the Joad family's journey from Oklahoma to California on their search for survival in the Depression as they traipsed through ruined landscapes, hobo jungles, and worse.

What one learned in, say, electrical, automotive, metal, or wood shop was pretty useful, especially when combined during sum-mer vacation with work with a master electrician, mechanic, or carpenter. The sorting process began in junior high to determine who would do manual labor, who would be in business, and who, if anybody, would go on to college and the professions—a process to be completed in senior high. Donald assumed he would undertake education beyond high school—his parents and grandparents had—but he very much also liked shop.

Just as it was a social and curricular sandwich between elemen-tary and senior high school, junior high shared familiar acts of mischief in class and after school. There was a new twist, though. The boys by this time had gotten bigger and rougher and were anxious to prove their physical prowess, either merely by besting another boy or by showing off before the girls. The socially elite, and better heeled, young fellows were tamed somewhat by means of the Floyd Ward School of Dancing, an activity that few boys longed for and many could not afford at 75 cents a lesson. Donald was one of the latter group.

Several new torture techniques came into being in junior high. If caught—a rare event—the perpetrators were likely to be sent to the principal's office for a dressing down.

One of these "fun" activities—if one may dignify it with such a designation—was the act of arm-socking between two boys. Here is what would happen. A boy would perhaps be a little tardy arriving in class—this was the first school level where students moved from room to room for different subjects rather than the teachers—and have to pass down a row of other boys to get to his seat. Somebody would trip him or smart-mouth him in some way. The reaction was instantaneous. Boy #1 would slug Boy #2 on the arm—hard! Boy #2 would immediately retaliate by standing up and slugging Boy #1 back on his arm. Later, on the playground or after school, it became a conscious contest between many pairs of boys to see how hard they could hit each other on the arm. In time, arm-slamming turned into stomach-slamming. You were okay if you could take solid hits to the belly while holding your abdominal muscles tight. Mothers were always inquiring of their sons why their arms were so red.

Another favorite activity of the boys was choking a pal. One guy would, without any provocation, wrap his arm around the neck of another and tighten up until the person turned very red in the face. Such brutishness usually took place on the school bus or in the school yard before or after classes.

And that is the way it was with one of the most inventive of all torture techniques. A group of boys would gather round one boy on the school yard and throw him down. They would then pull up his shirt and lower his belt line and while two boys held the victim down, a third would give him a "pink belly." Using two fingers held side by side the torturer would repeatedly slap the victim's belly in the area of the navel until the kid's belly turned bright red or until the kid yelled "uncle." All the while the boys making the curtain around the event—so as to shield their business from wandering teachers' eyes—would egg on the sadist at work. This kind of stuff often backfired when the tortured one managed to enlist the aid of some guys at a later date, who would pin down his torturer and give him some of his own medicine. Great fun. Mothers seldom learned of this ridiculous game.

What connection did such shenanigans have with the Depression? Donald, and every one of his cohorts, learned something about parental anger when returning home dirty and disheveled and with torn clothes. It was mostly the ripped clothes that evoked punishment at home. After all, few families had enough money even by now to put up with roughhousing that meant repairing or replacing perfectly good clothing.

Junior high was an educational stage best forgotten by all concerned.

Centenary Methodist Episcopal Church, South

CHAPTER 9

Church and Sunday School

Although long since a Catholic, Donald was raised a Protestant. This twofold experience has given him a wide window on both varieties of western Christianity. It might have been the other way around if he had lived somewhere else, but Lynchburg had very few Catholics and only one Catholic church. His only Catholic friend, Frank Callaham, was also his neighbor. This means that his exposure to organized religion in Lynchburg was based on the majority perception of church and Sunday school.

Expressed in the simplest of terms, the general perception then was that church and Sunday school were absolutely necessary to the proper upbringing of a child. This seems no longer to be the case either in the South or elsewhere. This assumption leads many parents today, Catholic as well as Protestant, to account for a myriad of social ills in terms of a lack of religious training.

From a theological standpoint, many religionists have criticized Sunday school as the most wasted hour of the week. From the precipitous drop in attendance throughout mainline Protestantism today—admittedly, with some decrease in attendance at Mass for Catholics as well—it appears that millions also think the church worship hour is wasted time. Donald did not see himself back then as competent to comment on the situation. Today he is very qualified indeed to discuss the theological and sociological problems at hand, but he will restrain himself and merely report, as always, what our hero lived through in the 1930s!

On a long-term basis, Sunday school and church were worthwhile because they provided religious facts, Bible verses, and the like, taught a wholesome message of social concern, and cemented an underlying sense of very useful guilt in children, as does the Catholic faith, too. The various summer Vacation Bible School programs, particularly the one at Dr. Graham Gilmer's Rivermont Avenue Presbyterian Church, provided wonderfully structured learning with clear-cut rewards over a lifetime. Short-term was another matter, as the reader will see from the account of behavior in Sunday school!

The schools lent tacit approval to a religious approach to life by not interfering with American traditions as based on the Judeo-Christian ethic. It would not have occurred to anyone to have the officially sanctioned recognition of God removed from library walls, statues, cemeteries, and currency. Textbooks made unhesitating reference to the part God presumably had played in the founding of this nation. During these days of economic depression, prayers both public and private were frequently offered. No criticism was ever forthcoming that Donald can recall.

In those days, most people in the South didn't use swear words; for one thing, the practice went against some people's religion; for another, to do so would incur the wrath of the local public as socially unacceptable practice. It wasn't that people didn't know the words; everybody knew them all. But to employ them would assure a youngster—and a lot of adults as well—ostracism from polite society. It was a cultural matter. Donald remembers the cloud under which a new neighbor "from up north" lived after he was once heard to utter the word "damn." Children, Donald included, sometimes had their mouths washed out with soap for swearing even a little.

Church and Sunday school and home all three contributed to the creation of an atmosphere of semi-piety. This attitude was most in evidence on the weekend, but the built-in guilt factor gave it impetus to some extent throughout the week. The oft-repeated slogan was: CMCLCTNL—Clean Manners, Clean Language,

Clean Thoughts, No Lies. Reminiscent of Boy Scout virtues, you would think Sunday school would be the perfect example of piety in action. Not so. And what about those boys (and girls) who didn't go to church or Sunday school? There were some, though not a lot. Did they bring out the worst in the churchgoing crowd? You bet. Well, at least that is what everybody said. Even back in those days people were reluctant to accept blame for much.

So what was a typical Sunday school class like at Centenary Methodist Episcopal Church, South? It consisted of about eight boys (or girls or mixture thereof). The real rowdiness began with boys from about 11 to 14 years of age. They didn't want to be there, and probably neither did the teacher, who was invariably a volunteer unused to controlling a mob while trying to instill some serious material.

One particularly capable teacher, a local lawyer named Ed Graves, became a good friend and encouraged Donald to attend Washington and Lee University. Donald had long wanted to go there, and Ed was both an undergraduate alumnus and a law school graduate.

There was a lesson plan all right, usually based on a booklet issued by the national church, but the boys always had other plans. They didn't want to talk about religion and sweetness and light; they wanted to talk about sports and other forms of mayhem.

One day the topic based on the scripture for the day had to do with giving to the poor. The concept was made current by reminding everybody that these were Depression times and that the poor were all around. This statement elicited much rancorous discussion because most of the boys didn't have as much as they thought life had entitled them to, and so they gave the teacher a very hard time. While the lesson was in progress, one boy was tossing loose objects of all sorts out of the open window. Chastised by the teacher not only for being obstreperous but for wasting perfectly good pencils and erasers by throwing them through the window, the boy simply got up out of his chair, raised the window higher, and climbed out. He was followed by two others, all of whom disappeared on a run over the adjoining Ruffner School athletic field. Donald was not one of these.

What is one to make of such a scene? At least two things. 1) Boys will be boys, though that is little comfort to the teacher. 2) There was little awareness of the suffering of others during this time because this city had, quite frankly, fared better than most.

Other classes were punctuated with loud talk, inattention, arm-slamming, and worse. None of the subterfuges utilized in school were employed in Sunday school. That is why the short term differed so greatly from the long term. The children had to grow up a bit and gain some perspective.

Behavior at church services was nowhere as chaotic as at Sunday school. Children of all ages were expected to dress appropriately for worship. For the boys this meant jacket, white shirt and tie, and shined shoes; for the girls, nice dresses and proper footwear. Parents would have been appalled to see children in dungarees, shorts, undershirts—now called tank tops, brogans, baseball or tennis shoes, and hair flying in all directions. "Dress your best for the Lord," was another catch phrase in vogue. Even those whose clothes were sometimes shabby appeared to have done their best to put a crease in their trousers and polish their shoes. The Depression had taught everyone to "make do" and maintain pride simultaneously.

As children got older and the sexes became interested in each other, some youngsters actually looked forward to going to church and socializing with a girl friend or boy friend. Sitting together meant reducing the strain of listening to a dull sermon; after all, young folks were going to live forever. What did they need all that religious talk for? As for their sins, which the preacher was probably screaming about . . . well, they weren't all that bad, were they?

Church and Sunday school exposure, ineffective as it may have seemed moment by moment, week by week, by so many, had the long-term effect of a vaccine, giving protection for the future against the invasion of despair born of job loss and consequent financial insecurity.

CHAPTER 10

Taking the Train to Georgia

‏In the 1930s the train was
utilized in the United States for long-distance travel much as the
airplane is today. It is now an unfamiliar, largely defunct means of
transportation except for some freight hauling and for commuter
travel between closely situated large cities. In fact, the author will
wager that very nearly 95% of today's youngsters have never been
on a train in their whole lives. Try booking train travel tomorrow,
especially to some small or medium-sized city, and you will find
it almost impossible to do so. Many tracks have long been torn
up and passenger stations abandoned, converted, or razed all over
the country.

Every summer Donald and his mother would travel by train to
Georgia to visit her family for about a month, after which Donald's
father would drive down for a week and then take everybody back
to Virginia. There were occasional other trips during the fall and
winter, but always by car. The reader may wonder how an entire
chapter can be dedicated to train travel to Georgia. Read on. You
may learn something.

First of all, it was a long time before the Southern Railway
acquired diesel locomotives, so Donald's travel was exclusively on
trains pulled by steam locomotives. The reader may think that
what was pulling the train cars should not make a difference as
long as one made the trip. Wrong from two points of view.

In terms of efficiency, smooth acceleration, and environmental-
ism, diesel and electric engines won out by the 1950s. In terms of
romance, steam engines have always carried the day. In retrospect,

Kemper Street Station. Opened on Oct. 31, 1912 and once served by 18 daily passenger trains, some bearing famous names

Donald was not sure how many people had, like him, actually ridden thousands of miles on trains pulled by steam engines. If they had, they might vote differently.

The trip to Georgia began with the family rising early enough to drive across town to the Southern station on Kemper Street by about 4:30 A.M. There was never a line, so it took no time at all to purchase tickets. Although there were two large waiting rooms—separate for white and colored—and a ticket office on the top- or street-level, actual departure was downstairs at track level. You could drive to this lower level and park if you already had your ticket. There were benches under a long roof for 200 or 300 feet along the tracks. Although it was customary to call ahead and ask if the train was on time, trains were seldom late in those days.

Donald stood beside the track and waited with his parents while looking to the north, listening for the train's whistle, and watching for the big headlight. (If Donald's memory serves him correctly so many years later, the train actually arrived in the station from the opposite direction.) As the train entered the station area, it made an enormous racket, hissing and pounding and clanking and ringing its bell. Everybody stepped back just a little more because you could feel the ground shake beneath you. It was said you could get sucked under the train if you were too close to the track. Steam seemed to be everywhere. (See the photo on page 68.)

And there was the engineer with cap and bandanna leaning grandly out of his engine compartment and waving to the as-sembled passengers below while pulling his bell cord. The fireman had stopped shoveling coal into the firebox, but you could see the red-hot glow of the goals as the engine rumbled by and lined up the passenger cars with the platform preparatory to taking on passengers. Two conductors jumped off the train, one at the door for entry of passengers, the other at the rear of the train. The first man announced in a loud voice, "All aboard!" Donald could see their bags being loaded into the baggage car up front. He and

Steam engine departing Kemper Street Station

his mother hurried up the steps to the tiny vestibule between the cars, waving good-bye to father on the station platform. Glancing back toward the rear of the train, Donald could see the conductor waving his lantern back and forth and heard the first conductor sound off again: "Boaaaard!"

Since Donald and his mother were to be gone for a month or more, two big bags were checked. Donald carried aboard one other small bag and a paper sack containing a lunch of fried chicken, tomatoes, bread, and a few grapes. At noon they would be able to buy a Coca-Cola, a Royal Crown Cola, or even an Orange Crush from a vendor who would briefly walk through while they were stopped in a station.

Mother had her cosmetic kit in one hand and her pocketbook in the other. They were about to sit down when the train gave an awful jolt. They had to grab for a seat handle to avoid being toppled.

In their seats now—Donald at the window, of course—there were more jolts to come. After the second jolt, the train actually stopped completely and began all over again. You see, in moving off from a standstill the steam engine propelled the train forward in huffs and puffs, each time causing the slack between cars to take up. However, in a few hundred feet the pace smoothed out, and as the train gathered speed, the passengers could hear the pleasant clickety-clack of the wheels on the rails as they clicked over the rail joints. Donald and his mother were on their way to Georgia. It will take them 12 hours to get to Gainesville, where Donald's grandfather will pick them up for the ride to Athens.

In a few minutes the conductor came down the aisle calling, "Tickets, please." With his official trainman's punch, secured to his belt by a heavy chain, he made a cross-shaped punch in the two tickets, put a copy of each in his shoulder bag, punched two little cardboard tickets, and stuck them on the seat back in front of Donald and his mother. He looked at his big watch and said in a friendly way, "We're right on time today."

It was so early Donald dozed off in a short while and didn't awaken until he heard the conductor announce, "Next stop, Danville. Danville, next stop." It was 6 A.M. as the train pulled into the station. Donald could see the big-wheeled, green baggage carts full of luggage being pulled up to the train by workmen. Steam was again coming out all around the bottom of the train, but Donald could still make out several people waiting to come aboard. He thought the train had stopped and had gotten up briefly to see better out of the window, when the train gave a mighty grinding sound and actually did completely stop, throwing Donald forward against the seat back in front of him. He then became aware of the panting sound of the engine when the conductor opened the car door and lifted the cover over the steps. A thrill a moment!

However, as the day progressed and got hotter and hotter, some of the thrill wore off as Donald and his mother battled cinders. On this particular trip it was their misfortune to be seated next to a window with a broken and torn screen that kept flapping in the wind. They tried covering their faces with handkerchiefs, but that didn't keep the cinders from blowing into their hair and eyes. Donald could scratch up black cinders from his scalp with his fingernails. In your eyes, cinders really hurt and were difficult to get rid of. Not much fun when you were also sweating like a Georgia mule, he thought. Donald had suddenly remembered the corny expression and laughed to himself.

During the early afternoon Donald got up and walked to the baggage car, where his mongrel fox terrier Scrappy was riding in a cage. The conductor had said it was all right to check up on the pet from time to time and make sure he had water and a little food. Donald found everything in order. While there, he looked around at the various bags and boxes aboard. The baggage master was sitting on a high stool at his desk against the bulkhead writing out some tickets or labels and attaching them to packages and pieces of luggage, which he moved into position for unloading at the next stop.

At one or two points Donald had to seek out the toilet, a fascinating contrivance situated at the very end of the car in a little closet with a door that wouldn't stay shut if the train lurched. Inside were a commode and a tiny sink. The water hardly ran at all, there was no soap, and the towel was a common one used by everybody and hung on a hook above the sink. When you flushed the toilet, you could see the tracks racing by below. Scary, but interesting.

Grandpapa was waiting in Gainesville at 4:30 in the afternoon and took tired passengers, dog, and bags in hand and loaded them into his car. Sometimes he met his daughter and grandson in Commerce, sometimes in Elberton, and sometimes in Gainesville. It just depended on which train they took. It was a 40-mile drive to Athens that took close to two hours no matter which town the train stopped at on its way to Atlanta.

At the time, Donald did not know it, but, to all intents and purposes, train travel had only another 20-30 years of survival. Now, some 45 years even later, there is no chance of its reinstatement to its former grandeur.

CHAPTER II

Visits to South Carolina and Elsewhere

ᥡAlthough the train to Georgia passed through parts of South Carolina where Donald also had relatives, he and his mother never got off and visited them. Instead, they waited until time to return to Virginia by car and stopped then. He visited Columbia, Greenwood, and places with strange names like Cheraw, Olanta, and Florence.

Young Donald was a close observer. Besides the people, he scrutinized what we now call the infrastructure—roads, buildings, telephone and telegraph lines, means of transportation—and compared it with that of his home state. Some things were the same, some were similar, and some were very different. What struck him first, and unforgettably, was the presence of roadside trash, shacks, and tumbled-down buildings, mostly in the country but also in certain sections of towns. To this day that is still the mark of the Deep South, southern Delaware, parts of northern New England, and Alaska—the trait of incipient or incomplete growth, of a social class gap, of racial or ethnic differences, of decadence, of outright laziness. Some of these factors were undoubtedly precipitated by the Great Depression.

As far as the last point is concerned, it is easy to understand why one would not want to do heavy physical work in the searing heat and high humidity in South Carolina and Georgia. Yet, there was no choice for farmers in the field, particularly during this time of severe economic downturn, where every bale of cotton, every bushel of peanuts or pecans, every ton of rice, every truckload of corn brought in money, meager though it was.

Donald noticed that the soil in north Georgia was mostly red, in south and central Georgia even redder. In South Carolina it tended to be very sandy. In central and southern Virginia it was both red clay and river loam. You notice this sort of thing when you ride around a lot. People in the Deep South had trouble growing nice lawns, but they had marvelous fig bushes and various kinds of fruit trees. There were also magnolia trees, chinaberry trees, and pine trees galore. The Depression years struck farmers especially hard if the weather didn't cooperate so they could raise and sell their crops. The warm weather was, however, a benefit for the average, non-farming resident, who could plant, and keep watered, a garden, a few fruit and pecan trees, and some berry bushes in his yard to supplement his diet.

The roads were generally two-lane and of asphalt or concrete surfacing. Curvy, poorly marked, unlighted, they looked nothing like the roads of today. Many roads and city streets were unpaved. Highway accommodations and restaurants were not very prevalent for white people and extremely scarce for Negroes. Stuckey's, founded in 1937 in Eastman, Georgia, south of Macon, was the one McDonald-like chain. It began as a pecan shop but later branched out to sell candy and snacks and even gasoline.

The one thing you could count on was unsightly billboards and Burma-Shave signs. The billboards advertised many different products and services; the Burma-Shave signs touted not only their brushless shaving cream but also provided humorous road safety tips and some good old-fashioned common sense. Here is how it worked. In groups of four, five, or six white-on-red signs spaced about 200 feet apart, low and close to the edge of the road, whole carloads of people would read and chuckle at such doggerel as these examples, with the last sign always announcing the product Burma-Shave: (With thanks to Candace Rich.)

The Midnight Ride
Of Paul for beer
Led to a warmer
Hemisphere
BURMA-SHAVE

Don't put your arm out
Quite so far
It might go home
In another car
BURMA-SHAVE

If hugging on Highways
Is your sport
Trade in your car
For a davenport
BURMA-SHAVE

All of those road characteristics could also be found in those days in, say, Texas or Arkansas or Nebraska or northern Michigan or Maine. Donald didn't know that then because he had not yet been to all those places. He admitted that an honest comparison with Virginia reflected the same inadequacies, just fewer of them. On a trip to the 1939 World's Fair, in New York City, by way of Washington, Baltimore, and Newark he had also seen narrow, and unpaved, roads. This was long before the New Jersey Turnpike and the Garden State Parkway. He also saw tremendous overcrowding, tenement houses, and plenty of beggars. The poor of the South could at least spread out.

Although residential telephone service was scarce compared to today, from the myriad visible telephone and telegraph wires—yes, there was still telegraph service—it appeared that every building had service. Nothing was yet underground, and the strings of wires in towns made every town look like a spider web. It was a different story in the country, where it often took years for electrical power and phone service to reach outlying farms. Of course, there was no sewer service either. Donald's grandfather's several farms in the Athens area were a case in point in the 1920s and the very early 1930s. That pattern was repeated at his uncle's farm in central Georgia until the early 1940s. The people had to have enough money to finance practically the whole project of power service if they were miles from a town and/or join with their isolated neighbors. Few had that kind of money. Donald's relatives relied on kerosene lamps and stoves and wood stoves for light and cooking. Slop jars were found in every bedroom, and one or two odoriferous outhouses were located to the rear of the house.

Most people did not own a car or truck but had to rely on public transportation. In many ways, it was more reliable than that of today. Buses and trains went everywhere. You could even safely hitch a ride with a stranger. If you forgot and left something of value on a park bench or a bus seat, there was a good chance nobody would steal it. Statistically, there was less looting than today. Why? Because the patterns of authority prevailed despite widespread need.

One thing Donald noticed right away was that the vehicles in the agrarian Deep South were older and had been repaired more often than those back home. Another curiosity: When they no longer would run at all, they were simply driven into a clump of bushes behind or beside the house and abandoned. That practice is still in force today in those same places cited above!

One year the family traveled to Niagara Falls and Ontario, Canada. Donald noticed less of the ravages of the Depression, but he did not see great progress either. The roads were no different from those at home, and the farms he saw on their way through that part of Canada looked very much like those in upstate New York, exhibiting an element of surprising shabbiness and little prosperity. The Depression was, after all, an international phenomenon that was perhaps too conventionally associated largely with the United States.

At least, that was his conclusion.

Scrappy in back yard at Ash Street house

CHAPTER 12

Wringing Chickens' Necks and Gigging for Frogs

ॐ Like the greatest part of the two earlier chapters, this chapter is set in the Deep South. The title describes two activities, the second of which could be called a sport. The first was not a sport but a necessary means of preparing food for the table. However, as far as Donald's dog Scrappy was concerned, there was a "sporting" angle to an activity that led to Donald's wringing a chicken's neck.

Even before the Great Depression, chicken was the favorite food of the South. No Sunday table was complete without fried chicken. For that matter, chicken was eaten on many other days of the week as well. It was eaten mostly fried but also baked, boiled, sautéed—you name it—and hot or cold, as a main dish, as a snack, or in a sandwich. Everybody ate eggs for breakfast. Chickens were a staple, no question about it. Things haven't changed much even these days.

Donald's grandmother kept chickens in the back yard of her house in town. She also had a hen house for her layers. The chickens were allowed to run loose throughout a big, fenced-in portion of a very large three-part yard. They scratched and pecked and clucked and moved around all day and at night roosted in the hen house, two other coops, and in nearby trees. On the farm five miles outside town they ran loose everywhere. It was often hard to walk through a yard and not soil one's shoes. Walking barefoot in the chicken yard was unthinkable. The chickens that ran into the road sometimes got hit by a passing vehicle; others were consumed by roaming foxes. The farm dogs paid no attention to the chickens.

Donald's dog Scrappy was usually kept on a line or permitted to run free in the second part of the yard only, well away from the chickens, although, when he first arrived, he had been allowed in the main back yard, where he quickly made friends with the colored girls from the farm who came to wash the clothes in a big iron, wood-fired wash tub. He played with the girls and seemed not to pay the chickens any particular attention. However, it was thought to be safer to put him in the other yard. One day he managed to invade the chickens' yard. What happened is not clear, but he started to race all about. Pandemonium. By the time he was through he had chased down and killed two chickens, one of them a prize layer.

Donald's grandmother was not happy, to put it mildly. She thought Donald needed a lesson: Not only would he have to help her pluck the dead chickens, he would have to make absolutely sure his dog never got loose again. Besides, Granny explained, even if the dog only chased but never caught and killed another chicken, the stress on the layers was such that they wouldn't produce their usual quota of fresh eggs.

But there was another part to his punishment. There was company coming, so he would have to catch and wring a third chicken's neck and then pluck it. It wasn't that he didn't know how; goodness knows, he had seen his grandmother carry out the process many times. He really didn't think there would be a problem.

There was. First of all, he did what he had seen his grandmother do. He scattered some seed and waited till the chickens gathered about and then grabbed one by the legs and the underside with both hands. With his right hand he began to wring the chicken's neck. It was much like cranking a car. After four or five cranks, as it were, he pushed on the chicken's body with his left hand and quickly pulled on the head. But it didn't come off as it always had for his grandmother, who would toss the head into a bucket and wait till the torso had stopped bleeding and kicking violently and then drop that in as well. Instead, the neck was stretched grotesquely. Not knowing what else to do, he picked up a nearby ax and severed the chicken's head from its body. Not a pleasant task, to say the least. His grandmother said the chicken had not bled properly, but she accepted Donald's work and dropped the chicken into the hot water on the wood stove. Donald was relieved that she didn't make him pluck it after all. The smell of boiling chicken feathers was dreadful.

Donald and his cousins had several chores when visiting their grandparents: chopping firewood and stacking it in boxes in the house, collecting the fresh eggs from the nests each morning, and seeing that the chicken houses were tightly secured at night. Donald made sure his dog stayed where he was supposed to be. After all, chickens were food, and not to be wasted. Even in better times Donald's family would not have failed to protect their chickens and livestock.

The children were also asked to pick figs and pecans from the bushes and trees in the back yard. It was then their duty to peel the figs and shell the pecans. For their reward they could have an extra share of both.

When the horse-drawn ice wagon came, they were allowed to give the order for the number of pounds of ice needed that day. After the driver had chipped out the proper-sized block of ice for the ice box and carried it into the kitchen with his massive tongs, the children could have the ice shards from the floor of the wagon to suck on. Really tasty stuff on a hot Georgia day!

Now frog-gigging was clearly a sport, but food was unquestionably the outcome of the effort. It was a sport for men and boys, never for women and girls. Normally, a city boy wouldn't know anything about gigging, but Donald spent part of his summers at his grandparents' farm and, in time, was even allowed to gig some himself. Here is how the process worked.

On some Wednesday or Thursday evening Donald and his Uncle Edgar and another uncle—and his father if he was there on vacation—would drive from town out to the farm together.

Fowler's Lake, c.1933

The family had two good-sized lakes on the property, one that was primarily for swimming and fishing, the other for fishing and gigging. During the summer months the swimming lake was open on weekends to the public for a fee, and the kids had a great time selling tickets at a little booth set up near the water. Swimming and fishing do not need much explanation, but gigging may.

The gigging party would arrive at lake side at late dusk and launch two rowboats. One or two men would get in one boat, and Donald and the other man would get in the other. The men in the first boat would have a pair of gigs, or fish spears, and a bucket or creel. In the other boat the other man and Donald took along a spotlight hooked up to a car battery.

Everybody listened for croaking sounds and shoved off in that direction. It was dark, so there was only the sound to guide the giggers. When the croaking became very loud, one man suddenly turned on the spotlight and trained it in the direction of the frogs. The men in the other boat then plunged their spears into the mesmerized frogs and dumped them into the bucket or creel in the bottom of the rowboat. The light was then turned out, and everybody waited for maybe five minutes till everything settled down again and croaking could be heard. The only light was that from the cigarettes that were being puffed in the interim. Suddenly, the light came back on, and the process was repeated. When the containers were full, the men rowed to shore, climbed out, and put everything back in the truck for the ride to Uncle Edgar's house on the farm, where the women cut the legs off the frogs and packed them in ice to keep until cooking.

There were occasionally times when the hands and tenant farmers were permitted to fish and gig at Fowler's Lake. Donald also hunted, during the appropriate season, for rabbits, duck, and deer. These activities, though fun in some sense, were also necessary to supplement the diet. Such privileges extended also to a few friends and neighbors, and the gift of a chicken now and then, some eggs, and even a box of biddies made life more bearable and enjoyable for all in tough times.

CHAPTER 13

Learning to Drive

&Donald had loved vehicles of all sorts ever since he could remember. Like all children, he began typically small by learning to ride a tricycle and a bicycle. (Does a foot-propelled scooter count?) Later, he easily conquered a motor scooter. But what he really wanted to operate was a car and an airplane. Trouble was, he was only eight.

He didn't wait for someone to teach him to drive; he taught himself a great deal by watching others, even though these were Depression years and the opportunities to ride in cars, let alone airplanes, were relatively few. Every time he would ride in a car, whether in his parents' or a neighbor's, he would carefully observe how one proceeded to start the engine, to move the vehicle forward and backward, and to stop it. He studied the dials on the instrument panel. He did the same when he rode on an interstate bus and later, a city bus, when they had replaced the streetcars. Occasionally left alone in his parents' car, he would shift gears over and over without starting the engine until he was completely familiar with the pattern. He already knew enough not to release the hand brake or turn the key. He frequently chose a seat just in back of the streetcar motorman and felt confident after a while that, given the chance, he could run one of those too! After all, there was no steering involved, just braking and accelerating.

From about age nine, on his family's farm in Georgia, he learned to ride horses and mules fairly well, to walk behind a plow pulled by a cranky mule, and to control a pair of horses or mules pulling a wagon. It was only a small step upward to drive a tractor across a field and into a barn. He knew that driving a car would be a snap.

In those days not all states required driver's licenses, and Georgia was one of the more casual states in establishing and enforcing that law. Just as now, in all the states, one could of course drive on one's own property at any age without a license, and that is how Donald began—at age 10. He drove on his grandfather's and uncle's farms and at his grandfather's house in the city, where there was lots of space. He did not do this alone, and without permission—oh, no, he had a couple of relatives and one older friend who were willing accomplices! What he did should be interesting to a young reader anxious to get behind the wheel of a car today. However, the reader should be aware that streets and roads back then were seldom crowded; in fact, you could often drive for miles and not see another car.

Billy Whitworth and his family lived in Donald's grandparents' house in a separate apartment created by closing off a section of that big, old, Victorian dwelling. Because of unemployment, the Whitworths had moved from Lubbock, Texas, to Georgia to find work. Mr. Whitworth was hired by a local laundry as a driver.

Donald and Billy were companions during the summer. Billy was about three years older and used to help his father deliver laundry. Each noon the old man would come home, eat his dinner, and take a nap on the couch. Billy would appropriate the keys to the laundry truck, and he and Donald, taking turns as driver, would go for very short rides back and forth along the side of the house and yard as far as the back yard and garage, turn around, and repeat the process. The trip each way was so brief the driver never even got out of second gear, but it taught both boys a great deal about synchronization of clutch and accelerator. One day Billy and Donald sneaked in an extra two hundred feet or so and slipped momentarily into third gear. Glorious!

Once in late 1939, on a trip out of town with his aunt, who was only 14 years older, Donald was permitted to drive her brand-new 1940 Olds coupé with Vacuumatic shift for several miles on a highway. All you had to do was give the gearshift lever a nudge, and it popped automatically into first one gear and then the next. Very, very modern in those days. Donald had practiced so much on the laundry truck, the family's Pontiac, and his grandfather's old Dodge sedan—which he had learned to crank with a handle—that his aunt could scarcely believe how smoothly they sailed along. When Donald's father came down to pick up the family for the return to Virginia, he allowed Donald to drive their car for a short distance. From then on Donald's father played the part of the driving instructor. But it was a long wait for Donald till age 14, when he could get a license in Virginia.

He did not relax his self-instruction and observed the operation of various kinds of vehicles, from cars to trucks and buses. In those days cars had only three forward gears, and everything was manual. Most vehicles were kept for years and years because it was too expensive to buy a new one. Automatic transmissions appeared much later. He noted that some clutches were tighter than others, some gear shifts had longer throws, some shift levers were on the floor and some on the steering wheel, and some cars had loud, unpredictable, mechanical brakes. The same went for buses, although he noticed that the driver usually had to double-clutch through each gear. Big trucks were another matter, with a wonderful array of gears. All of this Donald picked up by riding buses and hitching rides in town.

Even then he instinctively knew more about cars than many drivers. Once, on a ride home with Miss Helen Nelson, one of his teachers, he wanted very much to tell her that her big Buick was faltering because she had selected second gear to start at the top of Bedford Avenue, instead of first. But he wisely kept his mouth shut since she would be grading him in English all year.

He never got a chance to drive a bus with air brakes, and that was a grave disappointment. He watched and watched the bus driver but could not quite imagine what the pedal felt like; it went down so far so fast, and upon being released, produced the distinct sound of air escaping. Cool.

Dr. Plunkett's Cord

What was definitely not cool aboard buses in those days was the prevalence of tobacco chewers, for he who chews has to spit at some point. Swallowing tobacco or the juice is simply not done without danger of vomiting. Chewing tobacco was cheaper than cigarettes, cigars, and even pipe tobacco, but it was a messy substance. On every bus, city or intercity, there were signs: "Please Do Not Talk to Driver While Coach is in Motion," "Whites to Front, Colored to Rear," "No Spitting on Bus." The last is of particular interest here: You could fill the bus with smoke, but you were not allowed to spit on the floor.

Well, what would happen if you just *had* to spit? The chewer would tap the driver on the shoulder and point toward the front door. The bus driver would stop the bus and open the door briefly while the chewer spat a long stream of tobacco juice sometimes clear across the aisle to the street outside, where it landed with an audible splat. The driver would then close the door and drive on. Not many city women chewed, but a number of low-class types would dip snuff and have to get rid of the excess from time to time in much the same way. Both sexes became expert at spitting through the teeth, a slightly more elegant—if one may use that word in such a disgusting connection—way of unloading a mouthful. In hotel lobbies and some homes spittoons were available for this purpose.

Ever so often Donald would thumb a ride from town. He got to ride in some rattletraps but also some very fancy cars, such as Packards, Lincolns, and Cadillacs. His favorite was Dr. Plunkett's pale-green Cord, a low-slung, front-wheel-drive automobile. It must have cost a mint and was the only one in town. Donald bet it could go 100 mph, but he observed that Dr. Plunkett never exceeded the 25 mph limit on Rivermont Avenue, for the cops would stop a car doing even 26 mph and hand out a ticket for $1.00 (one dollar for every mile over the limit). The dashboard of the Cord, especially when lit up at night, looked like the instrument panel on an airplane. There were controls that Donald could not even identify. It rode like the proverbial million dollars and hardly made a sound. Donald would have mortgaged his entire life to own that car.

Donald thought, even better than learning to drive would be to learn to fly. However, that had to come later because that kind of license you couldn't get until you were at least 16, still a while away.

The reader may ask: What does all this about transportation have to do with the Depression? First of all, it is part of a running narrative of a boy's life during that period. It is also a reminder that cars were scarcer than today; driving was safer; buses and trains were the main means of distance travel; and hitching rides was neither dangerous nor unusual and also bespoke the generosity of many people who owned automobiles.

CHAPTER 14

Furnace-firing, Clinkers, and Lawn Work

⩗Aside from a number of unpaid chores around the house, Donald started working for his own money at age 10. It was at that time that his allowance ceased. There was a certain parental logic here: Since he was earning his own money, he did not need an allowance. After all, these were hard times.

Then there was Donald's logic: Since his allowance was small—50 cents a week, he needed to get a job if he wanted to buy those things that every boy longs for. It wasn't long before a revised parental logic took hold: Donald should save his money, not spend it. After all, these were hard times.

The end result was that he did indeed buy certain coveted items with his money and he did save a large portion of his money over the years. There could have been no better self-training during the Depression years.

Donald felt that many of his peers wasted money and time buying and trading baseball cards picturing famous players and bubble gum cards depicting horrible scenes from the Ethiopian War, with Italian soldiers stabbing people right and left or detailing the rape of Nanking, complete with explosions, fire, and distraught people. Some also managed to buy, from under the counter at certain drug stores, Little Orphan Annie dirty books. On these, some kids doubled their purchase price. Donald, on the other hand, spent his meager allowance to begin a new hobby: the raising of tropical fish. He got started when he found an old aquarium in somebody's trash heap. He made it almost good as new by recaulking it with some special black gunk—but it never completely stopped leaking!—and buying some fish through the Johnson Smith catalog.

But what could a 10-year-old boy possibly do to earn regular money? For one thing, the newspapers were always keen on hiring delivery boys, and some of Donald's friends delivered either the morning or evening paper—there were two dailies in those days, just as there were two mail deliveries Monday through Friday and one on Saturday.

Frank Callaham chose to bring the morning paper, and Dick Hoskins the afternoon paper. Frank walked his route. With his white Spitz dog in his handlebar basket and his papers in a saddle bag on the back of his bike, Dick faithfully made the rounds in the late afternoon. Both boys did their job alone; no parent chauffered them around even on rainy or snowy days. First of all, it would have been too expensive to use a car that way and secondly, parents would have considered such coddling unwise. If asked, they refused, saying that the postman, who delivered mail to each house twice a day, put up with rain, snow, and biting dogs. Another good friend, Joe Gray, also delivered newspapers, but being from out Boonsboro way, he served a different neighborhood.

Donald chose a job closer to home than delivering newspapers all around: He chose to fire furnaces. The idea came to him because he fired his own furnace. In the morning he stirred the clinkers, removing some to make room for the four or five shovelfuls of coal that he added from a bin next to the furnace. Throughout the day, while he was at school, his mother—or his father, if he was at home—added coal once or twice. In the evening he banked the fire for sleeping.

Next door lived two single women in separate apartments, one, a widow and nurse, with a woman friend, and the other, a divorcée with a young daughter. They agreed to hire Donald to look after their common furnace. Because the women in one side of the house were gone all day and the second woman was obese and unable to do any work, Donald had to shovel one more time during the day than at his own house. Luckily, it wasn't long before the women had the newest device installed: a stoker. This meant that Donald could fill the hopper once in the morning and once at night and forget about returning during the day.

Within months Donald's parents and several other neighbors purchased stokers. Donald's business immediately increased from one to five customers. This business bonanza resulted in his having to hire a friend, Nat Bowman, from across the street to help out. They would split the money.

Part of the job associated with firing furnaces was the collection and spreading of clinkers in people's driveways. Red hot, they were removed from the fire and placed in large metal ash cans. After they had cooled down over several hours, Donald and his business partner loaded the heavy cans onto a hand truck and wheeled them out to the customers' driveways, where they spread them and raked them out evenly, chopping up the bigger ones. In time, the clinkers made an excellent driving surface.

The twice-weekly garbage truck would pick up clinkers, but most people preferred that Donald spread them in the driveway and save paving expense. Besides, the clinkers had to be thoroughly cool before they could be set out on the curb. Unlike garbage cans, which had to have tight-fitting tops to thwart the roaming dogs, clinker cans could be left open. In those days there were no automated devices for lifting garbage cans, and the full-size cans were over three feet tall and weighed 50-75 pounds when full of clinkers. Each garbage truck had three workers: a driver, who stayed in the truck cab, a man who, ready to jump down at each pick-up spot, hung on the side of the truck, and a man who stood in and stomped down the pile of garbage in the truck and emptied the containers thrown up to him by the other man. Nobody was going to throw a 75-pound ash can full of clinkers seven feet in the air over the back of a stake-body truck. Any way you sliced it, it was a dreadful job.

The arrival of warm weather meant the demise of furnace-firing except for a few homes that kept the stoker going very low in order to heat household water. This meant that Donald had to find other work. It was logical to mow these same customers' lawns. Most of the lawns in the neighborhood were small by comparison with lawns in comparable neighborhoods today. Fertilizers and assorted weed killers were seldom available or used, so the grass didn't grow all that profusely. But cutting three or four lawns every ten days or so brought in almost as much money as Donald had earned firing furnaces.

Was Donald more industrious than most boys his age? It is hard to say, for almost all of his friends had some kind of job before or after school. It is also hard to say whether the Depression times and family monetary pressures inspired these youngsters to work so diligently. There probably was a connection. In retrospect, there is no doubt that such hard physical work was ultimately healthful. The fear of being without a job and money stayed with Donald his whole life and cultivated his habit of saving and skillfully managing money.

Boy Scout Handbook

CHAPTER 15

Boy Scouts

For Donald and his friends, becoming a Scout at age 12 had been a lifetime goal. In those days there were few Cub Scouts and, besides, boys were interested in "the real thing," in an outfit "run by men," at a time when boys were trying to break away from their mothers.

Boy Scout troops were often sponsored by local churches and headed by scoutmasters usually from that the same congregation. In other words, there was a close tie between the individual church and the national scouting organization. Promotion for membership took various forms. There was, of course, some national advertising and stimulus. The churches themselves urged their youngsters to join. Even the government let it be known that scouting taught valuable morals and helped with charitable work during these hard times.

Typically, troop meetings took place on Friday nights in a particular church hall. There was a formation, roll call, and a few military courtesies and marching procedures inculcated and practiced. A business meeting followed, with a treasurer's and secretary's report, general announcements of past and upcoming events, and some remarks by the scoutmaster apropos plans for the immediate future and perhaps some new national policies to be put into effect. At this juncture, time was often set aside for members to work on merit badges, take tests, and get their cards signed by a senior scout or assistant scoutmaster. The whole evening was then topped off with refreshments of doughnuts and hot and cold drinks and a rousing game of, say, Capture the Flag. In 1½ to 2 hours the boys mounted their bikes for the ride home.

On special occasions—national holidays, for example—the troop might form a color guard in a church service, march down the aisle, and sit together. On Thanksgiving the Scouts would distribute food to the needy; at Christmas they would go caroling; and on Easter they would be back in church. Approximately once a month the troop would take a hike of several miles. About every other month they would spend the night in the woods. Several times a year the troop would go up Candler's Mountain on a 14-mile hike, as recommended in the Scout Handbook, spending the night in the open and preparing all their meals. This meant that many could earn credit toward merit badges in hiking, cooking, camping, and certain crafts. An altogether wholesome venture throughout. Well, except perhaps for the dreadful open-air meals—undercooked baked potatoes, slurpy eggs, cold beans, and coffee that tasted like battery acid—that were prepared by those seeking their cooking merit badge and whose instructors then had to test-eat the mess!

Scouting very much helped to broaden one's friendship and activity base. Because troops were invariably made up of boys from various quarters, there were always some in a troop whom Donald did not know from school or neighborhood connections. New relationships led to new group activities, such as, shooting and hunting forays, swimming hole fun at Ivy Creek, and a long-lasting cardboard boat building project. Actually, the last-named activity involved the other two activities simultaneously.

Here is what it was all about. Boys' and men's shirts used to come back from the laundry well-starched and folded around a piece of gray cardboard about 10"×15". After saving a good stack of cardboard, it was easy to make a boat by gluing several of these sheets end to end and, once these had thoroughly dried, crimping the pieces together lengthwise to form the bow. The stern was made wider by gluing on a horizontal piece of cardboard. With the hull still open, watertight compartments were inserted crosswise, and all joints were then sealed by dripping on hot paraffin. Fishing weights were glued to the inside bottom to provide ballast. The deck, constructed of more sheets glued together, was laid across the top of the hull and trimmed and sealed with paraffin. Separate pieces of superstructure were fashioned and glued onto the deck. The whole ship then received a coat of gray paint and, when dry, was ready for floating on a lake, pond, or creek. Everybody had brought along his BB rifle and had a grand contest to see who could sink whose boat first.

Anybody describing Scouting would, however, be remiss if mention were not made of the snipe hunts that took place on overnight camping trips. Usually, the newest member of the troop was earmarked for the great privilege of going on the snipe hunt. After finding a clearing somewhere, older Scouts would carefully instruct the neophyte just before dark. The kid was handed a gunny sack and told to hold it open so that the snipe could run into it. They, on the other hand, would sally forth into the brush and trees roundabout and begin vigorously swatting the ground with branches in order to flush out the snipe. After a while, it got much darker and the kid left holding the bag no longer heard anybody around him. When he had become thoroughly worried, his fellow Scouts appeared suddenly with flashlights and rescued him from his stupidity. Actually, such an idiotic activity turned out to be superb training for fraternity initiation!

A boy's ultimate aim was to make the rank of Eagle Scout, though very few reached that pinnacle. Not many more made Star or Life, just below Eagle rank. The general pattern was to drop out after a year or so of Scouting, but even those boys gained immeasurably from the experience of group activity, obedience, service to country and church, and honest, moral, decent living. Donald stayed in three years and made Life.

The success of a troop depended very much on the character and dedication of its scoutmaster. Donald counted himself as most fortunate in that respect. The first troop to which Donald belonged, Troop 8 at Rivermont Baptist Church, had a scoutmaster, Earl

Law, who was attentive to most of his scouting duties but obese. As a result he seldom undertook outdoor activities with the boys. The troop to which Donald soon transferred, Troop 20 at St. Paul's Episcopal Church, had, however, a scoutmaster, Jim Munday, who was completely dedicated to extensive outdoor experiences and who instinctively knew how to inspire young boys.

Although a few boys might have sensed some ominous signs of war in the air in the late 1930s and early 1940s, most enjoyed the Scouts for the friendship and fun the organization provided. Those who, upon leaving regular scouting, became part of the Air or Sea Scouts continued to profit in many ways and, like Donald, lent their services in the Civil Air Patrol. Only later did they realize what excellent preparation the Scouts had been for military service. Being able to include scouting on one's résumé was also a big advantage when applying for a job or making application to a college.

CHAPTER 16

Beetle Traps and the Gas Company

꙰Despite the intimation, there is no connection between the two parts of the title of this chapter except that both were jobs that Donald undertook to earn money. Yet, it must be said that the jobs were similar in that they required miles and miles of walking every day and paid unusually well.

The U. S. Department of Entomology had run an advertisement in the local paper to hire someone to distribute Japanese beetle traps in the area, and Donald answered the ad and got the job. So did his friend Billy Bryant, but Billy, who suffered from all sorts of allergies, did not last long.

There had recently been an infestation of the pests. At the time he did not know the meaning of the word *entomology* and had to look it up. He discovered that entomology is that branch of zoology that deals with insects.

He first reported to a small office in the federal building downtown and was given instructions and several maps of the city. His task consisted in walking from house to house in test neighborhoods throughout one summer and asking residents to allow a beetle trap to be installed in their yard. After gaining permission, in a given area, he would return with a trap and place it in whichever yard, front or back, and wherever in the yard the resident requested. Exactly one month later he returned and emptied the trapped beetles into little cylinders for mailing to a government laboratory. He entered the number of beetles caught on his survey sheet and turned it in to the office downtown.

To some people, anyone carrying a credential from the federal government was a suspicious character and needed watching or avoiding. Donald often had doors slammed in his face. If somebody happened to be watching, say, from across the street and he tried that house next, that door would also be slammed shut. Admittedly, these brusque refusals usually came from people in run-down neighborhoods where poverty was everywhere in evidence.

Donald began his pitch sort of like this. "Good morning (or afternoon), I am from the U.S. Department of Entomology and . . ." That was enough for some people to shout, "No, I don't want any!" Others would scream out to unseen persons in the back of the house, "It's the guvmint!" At that, the door would slam shut, and two or three persons could be seen exiting the house through back windows.

But there were other reactions. For example, some people would immediately tell Donald about their need for money and food and ask that he intercede with the government on their behalf. It took a lot of talking on his part to convince these poor souls that he was in no position to help them get money or food. They would then reluctantly agree to let him place a beetle trap in their yard.

Donald will never forget one reaction. He knocked on the front door of a dilapidated house in a very poor part of town. A friendly colored woman came to the door and asked what Donald wanted. He was holding a Japanese beetle trap in his hand and explained that he wanted to place one like it in her front yard. The woman was absolutely delighted and remarked at the trap's beauty.

Donald was stunned; he had never heard anybody admire a beetle trap. To be sure, it was an unusual item: a bottle with a little green, metal, cap-like roof and four yellow metal fins hung on a 4½-foot metal rod. In the bottle was a liquid that attracted Japanese beetles; underneath the bottle and fins was an enclosed snap-on tray in which the beetles would be trapped.

Yes, the woman said she would allow a trap to be placed in her yard, but here was the deal: She would like one for her living room as well. Donald said she would not be authorized two. Despite the explanation as to the trap's purpose, she said it was so pretty that she wanted it inside; in fact, she thought she could use it as a floor lamp. When, after installing her trap in the front yard and returning in a month to check it for beetles, Donald could not find the trap anywhere, he knocked on the woman's door. She showed him the trap in the living room. It was tied securely to the side of the sofa but, of course, contained no beetles. The woman beamed. Donald picked up his trap and left.

The following summer Donald got a job with the Lynchburg Gas Company delivering bills to houses in some of the roughest neighborhoods the city had to offer. One of his beats was the red-light district, 4th Street and roundabout. He picked up his day's supply of bills from the downtown office by 8 o'clock and started out on his route. Most of the time it was routine. He would go from house to house, checking the number on the dwelling against the number on the bill and leaving the bill stuck somehow in the front door, either between the screen door and the jamb or under the front door itself.

Once in a while things didn't go so smoothly and the resident would come charging out the front door and demand to receive the bill in hand. Sometimes—and it was usually a woman—the person would claim a mistake had been made, that there were no gas appliances in the house, and Donald would be forced to report this to the office so that somebody with more authority could take care of the matter. On other occasions people would complain bitterly about the cost of gas, blaming the company, the Depression, the government, everybody. Donald had to take it.

Once a woman ripped up the bill right in front of Donald and threw it in his face. Another woman flung a glassful of water at him. Another was in tears and insisted on telling Donald how the Depression had ruined their lives and that she could not pay any more bills.

Over the months of walking around delivering traps and bills Donald had sort of gotten used to dogs nipping at his heels.

However, one day he heard a woman shout to her already snarling dog, "Get 'im!" With that, the dog ripped Donald's right pant leg and began to chew on his ankle, at which, quite naturally, Donald began furiously kicking at the animal until it let loose. All the while the woman was screaming, "You're killing my dog; I'm going to call the cops!" Shouting over his shoulder as he ran away, Donald yelled back, "I wish you would." He thought he would have a pretty tight case against this maniacal pair.

Donald worked a 40-hour week for the government and the gas company. The government sent him a biweekly check based on the number of traps he had set out and the number of beetles sent to the lab plus a basic amount for his constant walking. It averaged out at about 30 cents an hour, about the same hourly wage that he received every weekend, in cash, from the gas company, when he dropped by after completing his route on Friday or first thing Saturday. It seemed like a lot of money in those days.

He saved three-fourths of it, adding it to his grass-cutting and furnace-firing money. He decided life wasn't so hard after all.

1509 Parkland Drive

CHAPTER 17

War Drums

⊱Typical of many families back then, Donald's parents were in their middle 40s before they owned their first house. In late 1939 they purchased a lot on the best side of town for $900 and the next year set about building, at 1509 Parkland Drive, a brick Williamsburg colonial that cost less than $6000. If this seems like a bargain price today, it wasn't all that cheap in those days, especially for a man who only earned between $100-$200 a month. Luckily, prices of almost all commodities had remained remarkably stable for a very long time. But things were about to change.

Like everybody else who was alive on Sunday, December 7, 1941, Donald clearly remembered for a lifetime what he was doing when President Roosevelt announced that the Japanese had just bombed Pearl Harbor at 7:55 A.M. local time and that the United States was henceforth in a state of war with the Japanese Empire. It was called a sneak attack, carried out by Japanese carrier-based airplanes, even while representatives from the Japanese government were negotiating with their American counterparts in Washington.

It was a simple scene. The family had just returned from church and, as always while preparing Sunday dinner, turned on the radio. The President spoke of the act that "would live in infamy" and promised a quick military response. There followed an accounting of the destruction: the bulk of the U.S. Pacific Fleet moored in Pearl Harbor sunk or badly damaged, 188 U.S. aircraft destroyed on the ground, 2280 military personnel and

68 civilians killed, 1109 military wounded, numerous buildings and pieces of equipment blown apart. The next day, December 8, Congress officially declared war on Japan. Within a few days Germany and Italy declared war on the United States.

Even though Lynchburg suffered less from the effects of the Great Depression than many cities and towns in the United States, by the time of the Japanese attack every boy in town who had paid attention to his teachers, done his reading in history and politics, and listened to the radio began to think back over the last three years and recalled certain ominous signs.

First and foremost was the spread of the Depression throughout the world; secondly, the aggressive acts of Japan and Germany toward other countries; thirdly, the sudden realization that World War II had officially begun on September 1, 1939, when Germany marched into Poland without a declaration of war; and fourthly, the institution of peacetime conscription in 1940. When, shortly after Pearl Harbor, it became clear that there were now two massive opposing forces in the world, the Allies and the Axis powers, teenaged boys—Donald among them—wondered what it all meant and whether they would be called to fight. The prospect of going to war was both tantalizing and frightening. For their elders it was only frightening.

From 1941 until the defeat of Germany and Japan in 1945, life in the United States took on an entirely different coloration from the Depression years. The drum beats of coming war had become the sound of actual war. Jobs, particularly in the defense industry, became more plentiful; men were drafted; many women had to work to support their families. Everybody was enjoined to work for the war effort, to support those serving in the military, and to save for the future. Suddenly, there were reasons all around for striving, sharing, and saving. Whatever one did was "for the duration."

During this period the country began to ration certain foodstuffs, gasoline, coal, and other commodities needed for the prosecution of the war and the well-being of the people. There had never been rationing in the United States. Great Britain was the first nation to utilize rationing on a national scale during World War I, which system by World War II had spread pretty much throughout the world.

Youngsters noticed that chocolate and other sweets, butter, sugar, many favorite foods, and certain items of clothing became scarcer and scarcer. Once again, houses were kept cooler in winter. Clothes were mended and re-mended. As during the Depression, lights were regularly turned off to save electricity. Tires were hard to replace and recapped instead. Owners of automobiles were issued stickers A (the lowest in allotment) through D and cards to match that allowed them a specific number of gallons of gasoline per month. If one's work required the use of a car for travel, it often became necessary to go by bus if there was to be any gas left over for pleasure. There were other reminders that a war was in progress, among them, frequent air raid drills announced and concluded by screaming sirens, block wardens, blackouts—not even a cigarette could be lit, covered windows and hooded car lights, even arrests of those who dared not obey.

For some these rationings, regulated by the Office of Price Administration (OPA), constituted inconveniences, for others hardships. My father, who was a World War I veteran and who suffered from curvature of the spine, nevertheless was unable to get more than a B sticker even though his work required him to travel constantly. It always struck me as grossly unfair, especially since I saw neighbors' cars with C and D stickers, and I knew none of them had to leave town to go to work. Three weeks out of four, for almost four years, my father had to carry his suitcase in one hand and his heavy sample case in the other and take a bus to his far-flung territory throughout southern Virginia, not returning until Friday night. He also had to utilize bus transportation during the week, say, from Danville to Martinsville or from Farmville to Burkeville and Blackstone or from Lexington to Buena Vista and Glasgow or from South Boston to Clarksville and Boydton or from Waynesboro by way of Amherst and Lovingston, and other outlying places.

From the beginning of the war and for the next 15 years, my mother ran the C. K. Wilson Book Department in Baldwin's Department Store on Main Street. Like me when I worked at Millner's, she could not sit down all day except for 30 minutes at lunchtime. At least her bus ride was only on a city bus, but it wasn't easy bringing back bags of groceries sometimes at 6:30 at night when I was not at home to help.

Very few things were discarded. Cars and buses were being continually repaired. Bicycles were ridden more than ever before. People walked more. But despite some deprivations, people were no longer destitute. There were more jobs where they could work and earn money. The war rid the country of the Great Depression while inflicting different, and equally severe, woes worldwide. The word that Donald now heard everywhere was "the war," not "the Depression."

Three activities encouraged by the government and participated in by many of the populace were the raising of fruits and vegetables in a "Victory Garden," the keeping of chickens, and the renting out of extra space in homes.

Donald's family did all three. Their backyard garden contained tomatoes, squash, onions, spinach, turnips, peas, and lima beans. Closer to the house were several fruit trees. In the garage, which opened out onto the back yard, there were two cages with laying hens that provided fresh eggs. One side of the house had a separate small wing which the family rented out to a Navy man, Reno John Franceschi, who was in the recruiting office downtown. From San Francisco, he was of Italian extraction and introduced the family to real homemade Italian spaghetti, the sort of ethnic contribution to America that was multiplied many times during and after the war. But Lynchburg made him a contribution, too, in the form of a wife! Her name was Mickey Graves. Don visited them once several years later when he too was serving in the military in California.

As the war settled down to a sort of routine—it went on, after all, for four years—people also learned to live with practice air raid alerts and frequent blackouts and many other inconveniences and nuisances for the sake of the war effort. The Depression was over. If it hadn't been for the sorrow at the loss of life in the war, America might have rejoiced at its beginning a new prosperity.

E.C. Glass High School, with streetcar

CHAPTER 18

Senior High School

To aspire to high school back then in those days before and right after Pearl Harbor was natural, but relatively few persons, compared with today, reached that educational stage, let alone made it all the way through. College was an even less likely goal. The war gave those who didn't cotton to formal education all that much, who were characteristically unmotivated, a chance to opt out in favor of signing up for a stint in the military and still receive society's approbation. Since one high school served the white students of the whole city, and the three or four major sections of the city betokened fairly strict class divisions, the loss of a number of the intellectually indolent skewed the school in the direction of overachievers. The curriculum maintained the traditional three tracks called business, general, and academic, but there were more enrolled in the last category than in the other two combined. It included some who had little hope of actually going to college, but who, in the long run, thanks to the GI Bill, were able to make it.

In other words, the war had its impact. Early enlistments took some students away from further education altogether, but the war eventually made possible not only an education, both formal and informal, within the military but also one following service years. Some early enlistees were even able to return to Glass High before the end of the war.

Compared to most high schools today, Donald's was thoroughly conventional and offered to those in the academic track solid grounding in history, English, mathematics, lab science, and

Latin. The slots for electives were relatively few. Both the school day and year were longer, with fewer vacation periods, than what is normal today. The school's academic reputation statewide was good, and its football team formidable. Some maintained the school harbored a streak of meanness, but Donald usually chalked that opinion up to little more than rancor.

Not that Glass High didn't have a cadre of lazy, scheming students, mischief-makers, and sexually predatory types—all schools do—it was nevertheless more academically focused than the smaller county schools and some of those of cities of similar size. If there is truth to this statement, the reasons are probably based on the less drastic effects of the Depression on Lynchburg than on many other cities, the emphasis on academics, and a benign rigidity of local culture.

The first point made meant that the people of the city were spared the worst effects of unemployment and hunger, yet they remained ever mindful of national conditions. They were able to buy and enjoy more material goods, including books, than people in outlying regions, but they retained a sense of frugality and obligation to the war effort. There was little diversity in ethnicity in the high school, especially in the academic track and among those living in the two most prosperous sections of the city. This fact undoubtedly produced a social and educational inbreeding of academic usefulness. In other words, there was only competition between individuals, not an engineered academic and social leveling.

When Donald thought about the "benign rigidity" of culture, he did not have in mind the racial segregation that continued through the war years and afterwards. He thought in more general terms and would cite such values as obedience to the law, to parents and school authorities, and respect for morals. Parents kept their children on a shorter leash in those days, and schools reinforced the expectations inculcated at home. Not that students didn't break both home and school rules from time to time—oh, yes—but parents and school authorities worked in tandem to preserve order.

A simple example. There was Fielder's store directly across the street from E. C. Glass High, then located on Park Avenue, at which were sold soft drinks, candy, snacks, magazines, and the like. It was strictly forbidden to enter the store during school hours, but, of course, there were times when the temptation was just too great and students would sneak over, buy something, and sneak back. If they were caught by a teacher—not an infrequent occurrence—their parents were called and often summoned to the school office. And the parents came. They didn't argue with the principal, didn't express incredulity that their little darlings could have committed such a heinous crime, but read their kids the riot act when they got home. Further rule infractions were unlikely by those caught and chastened.

Donald remembers skipping the last five or ten minutes of a gym class once during his senior year and getting caught. Of the three miscreants, he was the last one over a fence and was, unluckily, spotted by the gym teacher. His two fellow conspirators had preceded him off the property. One, like Donald, was an excellent student; the other was more interested in mischief than studies. The code prevented Donald from ratting on his friends. The upshot was that, despite his exemplary academic record, he was summarily removed from the list of National Honor Society nominees; his friend was nominated and chosen. As part of the verbal lashing he received from L. H. McCue, Jr., the principal, he was told he "lacked character" and "would surely amount to nothing in life for having skipped [part of a] gym class." When he saw on CBS TV many years later, in 1984, a wayward, pregnant girl named Loretta Wort whose membership in the NHS was reinstated after she and her attorney successfully made the case that getting pregnant out of wedlock had nothing to do with her scholarship or, presumably, her character, he wondered about his school's "benign rigidity."

Perhaps a word about the cafeteria is in order. Unlike schools today, where the menu seems to be determined by the national habit of consuming quantities of burgers and fries and pizza pie,

Glass High's cafeteria food was thoroughly regionally determined. There was a variety of meats, often green and yellow vegetables, and always mashed potatoes. French fries had not yet become common, and pizza pie would not be known for another 15 years. Donald remembers complaining once to Mrs. Davis, the dietician, about the taste of a plate of mashed potatoes, how they seemed to be spoiled in some way. Mrs. Davis, very concerned, came over to his table, tasted his potatoes, mixed in the gravy a little more, and proclaimed they were fine, "just a little earthy." Donald's friend Herb was lustily putting down a plateful with his usual four peanut butter and jelly sandwiches brought from home. Mrs. Davis said, "See how he loves my potatoes?"

Drugs and booze were infrequently heard of in those days, but there was plenty of mischief, some of it benign, some not so benign. Consider a typical bus ride home after school. It was a regular city bus, not a school bus, and thus contained adults on their way to or from somewhere. They always cringed when they saw a bunch of high schoolers boarding their bus. So did the driver because at the very least it meant noise and disorder.

It also meant a lot of teasing and harassing of the weaker, less assertive students by the big, bossy ones. Slugging one another, grabbing books and papers and flinging them on the floor of the bus or out of the window were common, unpraiseworthy activities. When this kind of roughhousing was extended to the most vulnerable students, it took on an element of cruelty that repelled Donald.

There was a boy whose face was big and jowly, whose eyes watered, whose lips were large and loose, who drooled, whose knees knocked, who cried at the slightest provocation—obviously "afflicted"—that was the term then used—and who was frequently taunted. When the bus neared his stop, the meanies would throw Boyd Caldwell's books out of the window onto the pavement and call him "frog face." Of course, he began to cry and lash out at his tormentors. Sometimes the bus driver had to stop and walk to the back of the bus to quell the ruckus. The boy's mother, a perfectly normal-looking woman, would often meet the bus and help her son gather up his belongings and escort him down the street to his house on Rivermont Terrace. Some time later, the boy transferred to a different kind of school and was not seen again.

Every school has a few teachers feared and/or disliked by the students. Stentorian, but tin-voiced J. Heath Lewis was surely one of those. Mr. Lewis, a social sciences teacher, ran detention hall late in the afternoon and early on Saturday morning for the goof-ups, and that may be why.

But everyone can also recall a favorite teacher or two. That Mr. Abbott was everybody's favorite was indisputable. Uncle Charlie, as he was affectionately called behind his back, taught civics. By the time he taught Donald and his friends he was already ancient—or so he appeared to the students. He always wore brown double-breasted suits. His hair was mostly white, his gait was slow and irregular, and he had a habit of drifting off to sleep in class at his desk at the head of the room. He also smoked in class. A great opportunity for mischief.

Now it should be understood from the start that any mischief directed at Uncle Charlie was utterly benign, not at all comparable to such acts as putting tacks in Miss Glass's chair or giving a hotfoot to students in class. (For the information of the uninitiated but curious reader, a hotfoot involved surreptitiously sticking two large kitchen matches headfirst between the sole and the body of a boy's—no girl was ever given this treatment—shoe and quickly lighting the inert ends with another match. As the wooden matches burned down to the heads of the two sticking in the shoe, there was a sudden burst of flame and heat, and the person always let out a hefty yowl. He caught it at home too when the damage to his shoe was discovered. Of course, the kid reciprocated at his first opportunity.) One of the stories going around about Uncle Charlie was that he had the largest vocabulary of anybody in the school—he knew 40,000 words! It was only much later, when

Donald became a professional linguist, that he realized such a vocabulary was typical for a college graduate; therefore, he was sure Uncle Charlie's word stock was even bigger.

One day, by common agreement, two boys—Donald may have been one of them—arose from their seats in civics class upon noticing that Uncle Charlie was drifting off and went up to his desk. One of them carefully removed the cigarette from Uncle Charlie's nicotine-stained fingers and snuffed it out in his ashtray; the other lifted Uncle Charlie's limp hand off his book, laid it gently to the side, and folded the book shut. At that, the class quietly departed the room. It was shortly before bell time, so the students moseyed unobtrusively down the hall in the direction of their next class. When the principal was spotted heading for their classroom, the students' pace quickened. Donald does not know to this day whether Uncle Charlie got chewed out for sleeping in front of an empty classroom, but they sincerely hoped he didn't, for they liked him and actually learned a great deal about civics from him. Since no punishment was ever forthcoming, it is to be assumed that the old man rallied at the last minute and offered a plausible excuse to the principal, who was not beloved by anybody.

Of course, there were other good teachers at Glass and, in Donald's opinion, very few bad ones. One of the excellent ones was certainly Miss Elizabeth Glass, who taught Latin and inspired Donald to go into the field of foreign languages and linguistics.

Another who has always stood out in Donald's memory was a science teacher named Jack "Hop" Fielder, son of the storekeeper across Park Avenue and a private pilot and energetic promoter of flying. He introduced Donald to the joys of flying and gave him his first flight instruction in Taylorcraft and Piper aircraft at Preston Glenn Airport. Hop's earliest admonishments stuck with Donald all his life: "Maintain carburetor heat" and "A stiff neck has no place in an airplane; look around!" At his fiftieth reunion Donald was able to thank Hop personally for his inspiration and tell him a little about his two periods of service in the Air Force.

At that same reunion were many classmates, and it was good to reminisce. There were also some who were missing, including Don's very special girl friend, Dallie Bremer, who was killed in a single-vehicle accident 40 years before. Friends Nat Bowman and Billy Bryant were by now both dead, and John Taylor graduated elsewhere. But Lois Scott, Bev Lang, Polly Oglesby, Jane Edmunds, A. D. Thomas, Carl Douglass, Dewitt Beckner, Curtis Harper, just to mention a few, were all there and looking surprisingly young for all the intervening years!

During these high school years with the war as backdrop, the students did many good and proper things. They collected scrap metal, mostly without incident; they knitted all sorts of things—boys, too; they brought from home pieces of cloth of all descriptions to be sewn into quilts; they collected and mailed food, coffee, and trinkets for servicemen overseas; they participated in local clothing and food drives for shipment to civilians in Europe; they helped to maintain victory gardens; they attended patriotic functions; they conserved and preserved that which was scarce; and they did not complain, for they recognized their favored position away from the destruction of war.

But the question persisted: Was their favored position only temporary; that is, would the war last long enough that many of their number would be called up for military service?

Main Street, with Millner's Department Store

CHAPTER 19

Millner's Department Store

ℛThe next four chapters form a sort of unit describing the main occupations our hero undertook from the last year of the Great Depression essentially to the end of the war period and high school and the beginning of his college years. His experience in retail selling went on longer than the other jobs and thus was concurrent with whatever secondary or primary job he held at the time. Lingering memories of financial need during the 1930s prompted Donald to work after school and on weekends in order to add to his savings.

Founded by J. R. Millner and opened in 1890, Millner's, "The Shopping Centre," was Lynchburg's nicest and biggest department store. Donald was underage when he applied for the job of stock boy, but the floor manager took a liking to him and arranged for him to get a Social Security card, which would enable the store to hire him and pay in toward his retirement. This was an immense favor and one that led to Donald's receiving the biggest possible monthly social security check upon retirement some 54 years later. He is still receiving his monthly check and often thinks of Mr. Herbert Stork's generous act. Years later Mr. Stork bought old Thornhill's Grocery and turned it into an elegant dress shop called "The Avenue."

There were five departments on the first floor of Millner's: the cosmetics department in the center, the men's department on the right, ladies' lingerie on the left, and the ladies' handbag and leather goods department at the rear, just before the big door leading to housewares in the far back portion of the store.

The two elevators were located almost in the right rear corner of the first floor, just beyond the men's department. The up-down stairway was adjacent. Attached to the wall of the first landing was the time clock that employees had to punch upon beginning and ending their day.

The stock boy was at the beck and call of every department on the first floor. He therefore had to be thoroughly familiar with the location of the stock belonging to each department, which was housed in the back part of the basement of the building. Sometimes Mr. Stork would tell him to bring up one or two boxes of this or that, and sometimes one of the clerks would send him down for something specific. When he was not being sent off on a particular task, he stood around, sort of like a floorwalker, at the end of the cosmetics counter and waited until he was summoned by someone. He was usually pretty constantly on the move.

At the end of the day, it was his job to pick up the cash register receipts for the day and take them upstairs to Miss Myrtle Goggin in the store office on the 4th floor. Donald appreciated the trust placed in him, for there were hundreds of dollars in the five pull-string felt bags that he carried in a basket. Each Friday he would bring back downstairs from the office the pay envelopes for the first-floor employees and distribute them. Again, he felt honored and trusted. For his services, his envelope contained $0.25 per hour times the number of hours he had worked that week minus his contribution to Social Security.

After about a year Donald was so familiar with all the operations of the first floor that he could help customers when there was no clerk around. He recommended shirts and ties from the men's department and occasionally even suggested make-up and perfume in the cosmetics department. At Christmastime he wrapped packages for customers at a special counter set up by the store.

Soon Mr. Stork noted Donald's industry and gave him a regular clerking job in the men's department. He now walked the two miles from school to the store five days a week, instead of the previous three, and worked all day every Saturday. During the summer he worked full-time. It wasn't long before he was earning $12 a week.

Working, especially in a big store where people come and go all day, was more than merely earning money, although that was the biggest draw. It was an opportunity to learn how to deal with all sorts of people, not only one's fellow clerks but also the public at large. Donald used to straighten his stock on the counters and aisle tables only to have a customer fling everything this way and that while looking for a particular color or size. It was maddening. You would have everything neatly displayed, and someone would come and turn everything upside down.

Or, take returns. The store had a reasonable policy that it would take back anything bought there, as long as it hadn't been worn and the customer had his sales slip. Most people came properly equipped to get a refund. But some would become abusive when Donald would point out that the shirt or underwear had been worn and even soiled. It was then time to call the manager over to settle the matter.

The work day began at 8:30, but the store did not open until 9:00. There was a 10-minute break during the morning and one of the same length in the afternoon. Lunch lasted 30 minutes. The store closed at 5:30, but the day did not end for the employees until about 6:00. Throughout the day, except for your breaks and lunch, you had to stand or walk about. No sitting was allowed at any time, even if there had been any chairs or stools available. As far as Donald can remember, no one complained about the hours or having to stand all day. Everyone there had survived the Depression, been out of work at some time, and now counted himself lucky.

Most nights Donald rode the bus home. But some nights he got a ride home with "Tid" Barnard and her husband Fred. "Tid" worked on the 3rd floor and lived next door to his house on Parkland Drive. Sometimes he hitched a ride with his friend Billy's father, Lynn Bryant, who operated Webb-Whitaker, a men's clothing store down the street. "Old man" Haskins, who also

IN LYNCHBURG --

it's

MILLNER'S
THE SHOPPING CENTRE

for

HI-SCHOOLER FASHIONS

for Young - Men and Women

who are fashion minded

FOR YOUNG WOMEN

HI-SCHOOLER FASHIONS - THIRD FLOOR
JUNIOR SHOP - SECOND FLOOR
COLLEGE SHOP - SECOND FLOOR

FOR YOUNG MEN

BOY'S SHOP - DOWNSTAIRS
MEN'S SHOP - STREET FLOOR

worked at Webb-Whitaker, rode along most of the time and told the same story every night about "an old man farting in a jug." Donald never understood the point.

Other times, especially on Saturday night, he rode with "Fitch," an older fellow clerk in the men's department, and her husband and two or three other people. They would stop briefly at the ABC store and pick up a fifth in order "to get tight" over the weekend. During the week sometimes, Donald would pop over to the drug store and ask for a bottle of elixir terpin hydrate of codeine for her to sip during the day. He never knew whether it was a cough she was treating or a habit. But it didn't matter.

It did matter, however, when the department manager, Bill Williams, committed suicide overnight. It shook up the whole store. The day before, Donald had asked him why he was limping, to which he replied, "I just got tired of walking the usual way."

But most people Donald worked with were friendly and sane and committed to putting in a long, hard day for a small, much-needed salary. Besides, not long ago there had been hard times. These were changing times, times of understanding and patience. Times could get worse overnight. It had happened before.

With Richmond moving steadily out into the suburbs during the 1950s, the city's biggest and best department store, Miller & Rhoads, decided to expand into Lynchburg, Charlottesville, and Roanoke beginning in 1956. In 1960 it acquired Millner's. Like Miller & Rhoads in the capital, Millner's had played a major business role in the community, and though Lynchburg's branch of M & R performed well for quite a few years, many claimed it was not the same as the "hometown" store.

Former Gould-National Battery Factory, photographed by the author, 2003

CHAPTER 20

The Battery Factory

꙰The story goes that Lynchburg had the chance back in the 19th century to become the major rail center for central and southern Virginia but turned down the offer because the city wished to remain small and relatively free of industry. If true, the city lived to regret that decision because Roanoke acquired the railroad shops and thrived quickly. It should be added that this is probably a myth because there was much geographic logic in choosing Roanoke; there simply was not enough flat land to accommodate railway shops and switching yards anywhere in Lynchburg.

The years that followed produced other offers of industry, some of which were turned down—and maybe for good reason. But somehow, one day, Lloyd Howard, a member of the Chamber of Commerce, persuaded the Gould-National Battery Company to build a new plant in Lynchburg for the manufacture of automotive batteries. He later became their plant manager and made a great success of the business. Upon reading their advertisement for help, Donald applied immediately. He was hired on the spot.

National Battery Company was an outgrowth of Electrical Manufacturing Company and had acquired the Gould business in 1930. The origin of the Gould company name dates all the way back to the late 1800s. Charles Gould, who was a 35-year-old customs collector in Buffalo, New York, in 1884, purchased a small forging operation which produced couplers for railroad cars. In 1898 he established Gould Storage Battery Corporation, building on the patented electrical innovations of a polarity regulator, volt-

age regulator, and lamp multiplier. National Battery Company
was renamed Gould-National Batteries, Inc. in 1950. This joint
company pioneered work in sealed-cell nickel cadmium batteries, helping to create eventually a huge market for rechargeable
appliances of all sorts.

Donald had finished high school just nine months after the war
ended and the Occupation began but had not yet volunteered or
been called up for the draft. Even though he entered Washington
and Lee University on a $600 scholarship, two years later trans-
ferring to Emory University in Atlanta, he needed a lot of extra
money. In comparison with what he earned at his other summer
and part-time jobs, the pay at the factory was somewhat better—35
cents an hour plus occasional overtime at 50 cents an hour—but
the work was hard, at times dangerous, and boring. The factory
had little trouble finding people to work, though, because people
in those days were still grateful to get a good-paying job.

The work day began at 7:00 A.M. when a whistle blew at the
factory. All employees had better be there and ready to start
work or else they could expect to be fired. Since he wanted to eat
breakfast, Donald had to get up at 5:30. His mother was already
in the kitchen. He left the house in one hour because it was a
30-minute drive to the factory. By this time he had his own car, a
used 1937 Chevrolet coupé.

Working in a factory, Donald discovered, was very much like
being in the military. Everything was strictly regulated. You were
not allowed to goof off; you could not sit down; you had to ask
permission to go to the toilet or on break; you had exactly 20
minutes for lunch; you could not end the day one minute sooner
than quitting time.

Donald had a major job and a minor job at the factory. His
major job was making bottomless cardboard boxes of various shapes
and sizes to fit over the finished batteries. Though manufactured by
Gould-National Battery Company, the batteries carried all sorts of
names: Sears Die-Hard, Atlas, Delco, Montgomery Ward, Western
Auto, Goodrich, and Goodyear. Like most people, Donald was

not aware that so many different brands were actually made by one company. The old saying, "A battery is a battery," apparently held true.

The boxes were made in the following way. There were stacks of flat, heavy cardboard sheets, crimped at various places for folding to fit different-sized batteries. Two heavy-duty stapling machines stood side by side. Donald operated one, and his partner the other. For hours on end the two workers reached for cardboard sheets, folded them, inserted each end and side by turn into the machine, and stepped on a pedal that activated a press that plunged a one- or two-inch heavy, steel staple into the cardboard, making sharp edges all around. The boxes were stacked high around the machines. Every minute or so someone from the assembly line would step over and grab the proper- sized box and drop it over a battery moving along the conveyor belt.

Everybody worked very fast. Donald and his partner could turn out boxes like lightning, twirling them round and round under the press while talking to each other. It was rare that the assemblyman on the line had to yell out, "More boxes!"

One day, completely without warning, it was Donald's partner who screamed loudly; he had by mistake, in his hurry perhaps, stapled his left hand to a box he was making. He drove a two-inch staple all the way through the palm and back of his hand and the cardboard. Everybody on the line stopped work and ran over. Somebody dashed for the office and reported the accident. The boss called an ambulance and administered first aid, but the pain and damage were severe and the bleeding profuse. Donald cut the stapled box away from his partner's hand and comforted him while waiting for the ambulance crew. The young man was rushed off to the hospital. The last thing the boss said to him was, "You'd better be here tomorrow if you want to keep your job." He didn't make it back the next day, but he was there the following day, his hand completely swathed in bandages. He did his work with one hand. The injury took weeks to heal completely. The scars no doubt remained for a lifetime.

The other job Donald was assigned to was pouring acid into the batteries. For this task one normally wore a heavy apron, goggles, and gloves. Standing on the assembly line, Donald waited as each battery came slowly moving his way. When a battery was directly in front of him, he stopped it momentarily with a foot pedal, dipped a large syringe into a vat of sulfuric acid, sucked up a container-full, squirted acid into each cell of the battery, popped on the proper plastic caps, and hit the pedal to move that battery along and bring up another. Over and over, hour after hour. It was tiresome, dangerous work. You had to be ever vigilant that you didn't spill acid on yourself or anybody else and that you didn't breathe in too energetically. One night at supper Donald looked down in his lap just in time to see half of both pant legs disintegrate!

There were other jobs in the factory: case making and stamping, addressing and shipping, stacking and storing. Everybody agreed that pouring acid was the worst. It should have paid more than the other jobs, but it didn't, and most people were not in a position to turn down any job. There was no union here, so everyone was on his own. These were better times, to be sure, but they were not easy times. The day had begun at 7:00 A.M.; it ended at 6:00 P.M. It was 6:30 when Donald got home. Sometimes he was so tired he lay down on the living room floor and fell fast asleep without supper. It was one of the most physically exhausting jobs he ever had.

Donald worked an entire summer at the battery factory and then moved on to other job experiences.

CHAPTER 21

The Newspapers

ƎƷDonald, now often known simply as Don, had already begun work at a local mortuary, described in the next chapter, but he was convinced he could handle two jobs at once and double his salary. Here is why he was sure he could do that.

At that time there were two newspapers in Lynchburg, one a morning paper, the other an afternoon daily. The people who worked for the morning daily and Sunday paper, *The News*, generally came to work between 3:00 and 4:00 P.M. and stayed until midnight, when the paper was "put to bed." Those who worked for the afternoon paper, *The Daily Advance*, put in a normal day— 9:00 to 5:00. Proofreaders had a slightly longer schedule. Those who read proof for the morning paper worked from 5:00 P.M. until 1:00 A.M. the following day; the day proofreaders had a normal day. All of this meant that Donald could work for one of the papers at night and for the mortuary during the day, and vice versa.

His first job was as night proofreader. Back in those days there were no computers, so everything was set in hot lead and by linotype machines. Long galley sheets were printed out, proofread, returned for corrections, and then read one more time before final setting.

There were three proofreaders—two women and Don. They were seated on stools at a sort of old-fashioned, long, metal desk, with a sloping surface and two shelves and three pigeonholes above. On the right-hand side of the desk was a big, sharp, pointed hook on which the galleys were hung by the copy girl, who moved

The News and *The Daily Advance* offices (left foreground), with Allied Arts Building (in background)

constantly from the composing room to the proofreaders' desk to the city editor's desk for headlines, and back again. This process went on for hours and hours until all corrections had been made and the finished paper appeared on the desk. By that time it was usually nearly 1:00 A.M., and the presses downstairs were running full-time. Everybody had a deadline, and any holdup was costly. You were constantly being admonished to move along with your work. Any breaks had to be taken one at a time. Everybody had eaten supper before coming to work; you ate breakfast when you got home.

The reader may think this was a boring job. Not at all. Not only did the proofreaders get to read the whole paper every day, they had the power to correct all sorts of things. Primarily, their task was to check spelling, punctuation, and syntax, but poor style sometimes became a barrier to understanding, and they were expected to remedy that fault. Sometimes they confided in each other; sometimes they sought the city editor's advice. To make too many changes was catastrophic to the setting process and invariably called forth the wrath of the typesetters.

Proofreaders were decently educated people whose vocabulary had become immense over the years. In fact, it was a game, a goal, of theirs to acquire as many words as possible. Many of them did crossword puzzles in their spare time.

A good proofreader had to be an extremely close observer. To miss an error in spelling or punctuation, especially in a headline, could put the paper's reputation in jeopardy and possibly even call forth a law suit. Proofreaders prided themselves on their work. You fretted for days if you discovered an error in the finished product.

The following summer Don was hired as a reporter for the afternoon paper. There were completely separate staffs for the two papers, although the entire operation was housed in the same quarters. One wrote for one or the other paper, but occasionally one's pieces would be picked up by the other newspaper since both papers were owned by the same corporation.

A rookie reporter did mostly routine stuff—school news, traffic reports, town meetings, and the like. If he proved himself to the city editor, he might then be given a feature story or so, with his name on the "by line," complete with pictures, which he had to take himself, with the newspaper's big, expensive cameras. Again, everything had a deadline, and Don often found himself rushing back to the office to type up his reports and stories in time for the noon typesetting. Press run was at 1:30, and everything had to be approved and then proofread and, if necessary, corrected. There was a wonderful frenzy of work for those middle two hours in the day. After the paper was put to bed, Don could concentrate on writing up a special assignment or go out for an interview scheduled to appear in the next day's paper. The trite saying that newspaper people have ink in their blood was not lost on young Donald.

Shortly before returning to college, Don chose the Great Depression as a topic for investigation and research for a feature article he hoped to write. He began by checking in the newspaper's morgue, a repository of newspaper articles published in years past, and cataloged variously by subject, author, date, etc. He then went to the local library and read a number of books just appearing on the subject. He assembled enough of his material to conclude that his own on-the-spot impressions throughout those years had been largely accurate.

Indeed, he learned that Lynchburg did not suffer to the extent other cities of similar size had during the years 1929-1941. Unlike some communities that were more intent on preserving tradition, in all its good and bad aspects, the city fathers concentrated on preserving fiscal responsibility at all costs. Lynchburg, because of the Virginia law, remained as a separate city, with its own government, and not a part of any of its surrounding counties. No banks collapsed, and the city made good on its bonds. Could it have done all of this without the New Deal? Probably not. But there were many cities throughout the nation that had New Deal assistance and did not remain financially solvent.

CHAPTER 22

The Mortuary

In looking through the want ads one day Don ran across an ad for someone "with a strong back and a driver's license." Interesting, even tempting, he thought, and since he had both requirements, he applied for whatever job it was.

His interview was with Henry Cheatham, the new owner and president of Fauber's Chapel, a local funeral home, who was in need of an ambulance driver. Other duties included driving the firm's other vehicles: a second ambulance called a combination (meaning combination ambulance and hearse), the funeral car, and the flower truck. Under the law, and as a condition of employment, the person hired would also have to be apprenticed to the owner as a junior assistant funeral director and embalmer in training. It all sounded just right to Donald. When a call came accepting him the next day, he jumped at the chance to do something quite different. Besides, he was a pre-med student in college, and this kind of work seemed right down his alley.

The staff consisted of the president, Henry Cheatham, his wife Bonnie, who served as chapel organist and floral designer, Donald, two other men, and a janitor. Everybody was young, including the boss. Two had recently returned from military service in World War II and were anxious to get started on their careers. One of the other two men had been a friend of Donald's in high school. No one except the president held a full funeral director's and embalmer's license. All the others first had to undergo one to two years of apprenticeship.

Fauber's Funeral Chapel

The enthusiasm of this crowd showed most clearly in their fervor to respond to ambulance calls. In competition with the other mortuaries in town, Don and his comrades would listen to police calls over a short wave radio in their lounge and, if it was Fauber's "police month," rush to the scene of the accident. Of course, the police would also telephone the funeral home, but by listening to the radio, the guys could get the jump on the competitors, Diuguid's and Whitten's.

Sometimes the competition got nasty, and more than one company showed up at a wreck. This inevitably produced rancor. Donald was in the midst of things when there were heated arguments and struggles over who was to get the patient or the body. Downright gruesome at times. Once another company had to drive a body over to Fauber's that they had taken away without authorization. The boss was heard to remark more than once that he longed for the day when funeral homes would not make ambulance runs but only death calls. Of course, that is the way it is nowadays.

Some people would have been sorely disappointed if the ambulance calls had been done away with. They loved the excitement of flashing lights, loud sirens, and high speed. At any such place of business there are hangers-on, what are now called groupies, who like nothing better than to be around mayhem. Although not exactly wise to do so, the boss used to let us cart around one particular fellow named Louis Pank, whose love of ambulance rides was legendary. Only trouble was he could be a nuisance. Yet there were times when all of us and both ambulances were so busy that we needed an extra man. Louis was there and waiting to jump aboard. He could lift all right, but all too often he became squeamish at what he witnessed. He was absolutely useless in the embalming room.

This was the place that offered Don the most challenging experience. He learned how to remove the blood from a dead body, aspirate the cavities, and inject the embalming fluid. There were other things to know: how to sew up the mouth and glue shut

Aerial view of Fauber's, corner of Rivermont Bridge and D Street

the eyelids, how properly to massage the body when rigor mortis made work difficult, how to dress a body, how to apply make-up, how to clean up after an autopsy, and a myriad other things. He also learned what to say, and what not to say, to the grieving relatives. He learned to watch and not to talk when the boss was making a sale, even when the latter might be surreptitiously switching the numbers behind his back in a price stand on top of a casket in the casket room. He learned what to do at funerals and wakes. He learned what to do at Orthodox Jewish funerals. And everywhere that he learned what to do, he also learned what not to do. A valuable piece of instruction.

One of the things he and Lindsay Butler, a fellow apprentice, probably shouldn't have done was scare the daylights out of a teenaged colored boy who worked as janitor and general handy-man around the mortuary. His main duty was to keep the vehicles sparkling clean and waxed. This meant he spent a lot of time in the basement garage. When we returned from an ambulance or death call, he was there to help unload the vehicle and change the sheets on the cots.

Late one day, our appetite for mischief having been whetted by an embalming room trick we had played on this unfortunate boy several weeks before, Lindsay and Donald concocted a diaboli-cal scheme. Having just come off a death call, they backed the combination into the garage and unloaded a body. "Charlie" was watching but suddenly disappeared outside. He didn't like being around dead bodies.

After quickly running the body upstairs on the elevator to the embalming room, Donald and Lindsay returned to the garage, but this time Lindsay was lying on the cot all covered up with a sheet. Donald called out to Charlie to come give a hand; he was to take the "body" up to the embalming room while Donald finished backing the combination into the garage. Charlie re-appeared very reluctantly and wheeled the cot onto the elevator. To this day Donald can still hear the scream rocketing down the shaft. He knew exactly what had transpired: per agreement, Lindsay had

started to moan and rear up under the sheets between floors. The boss heard the ruckus and, meeting the elevator on the first floor, saw Charlie leave the building on a dead run over the D Street bridge to his house. After Charlie's father came to Cheatham and complained, Don and Lindsay caught hell. It's lucky they weren't fired, although they noticed that their boss had been laughing with them at first. (Not long thereafter, the boss lost his hairpiece in a heavy wind in Rivermont Avenue while directing funeral traffic at the home. The apprentices didn't let their laughter show, else they surely would have been fired!)

Don worked off and on nearly three years at Fauber's. During two of those years he had other jobs as well. Sometimes the work was very tiring, but all the time it was very interesting. Some days he worked all day at the newspaper and then went to work at the funeral home for 24 hours. Every other weekend he was on duty at the funeral home. For some of those hours he was sleeping in the home while on call, but scarcely a night went by that he didn't have to leap out of bed at least once, hurriedly get dressed, dash downstairs, and roar off on an ambulance or death call.

The Depression had no effect on the funeral business except to lower prices generally during the late 1930s and very early 1940s. After all, everybody had to be buried or cremated. By the time Don worked for the company, however, the economy was booming, and many people could afford even lavish funerals.

CHAPTER 23

The War and Its Consequences

ﾞﾟWorld War II changed a great
many things in America. It caused boys to grow more quickly to
manhood. It satisfied the romanticism of many, but produced cyni-
cism in just as many others. It accelerated marriage, often between
individuals ill suited to each other, and it upped the birth rate. By
drafting the father, it inconvenienced families just beginning to
settle down to a productive life. It devastated families when the
father—and sometimes the mother—was killed in the war.

But the war finally rid the economy of the effects of the Great
Depression when nations increased their production of war materi-
als. During the conflict there was work for all, and new products
galore. With victory in 1945 came also a renewed economy in all
aspects—banking, housing, automobiles, household appliances,
you name it—as large amounts of money flowed back into circulation. The government took increasingly greater responsibility for
bolstering the economy.

With national victory, however, there was occasionally individual defeat and disillusionment. Soldiers, sailors, and airmen
returning home sometimes failed to adjust promptly to an old
life they had been longing to resume during their years of service.
They had married quickly and now had to get to know their wives
and their children, some they had perhaps never met. Many were
lacking in education and had trouble finding and qualifying for
satisfying work. Many immediately entered college on the G.I.
Bill. There were those who resented having had to lose so much
time in the service while others claimed 4-F status and had gotten

ahead. Some veterans felt that civilians did not understand what they had gone through. Many civilians did not, in fact, understand them at all. This caused both groups to shrink from each other and to seek friendships among those to whom they could more easily relate. These "better times" suddenly became harder times in a social sense.

When World War II was followed seamlessly by the Occupation, the Korean War, and the "Cold War," the effects of World War II receded even as had those of the Great Depression.

But no war and no depression of the magnitude of the Great Depression, clearly the worst and longest period of high unemployment and low business activity in the 20th century, should ever be allowed to fall from the memory of any participants still living, whose duty it is to recount these experiences to the young.

Index

To receive a signed paperback copy of this book, send $12 by check or money order (includes S&H, no sales tax in Delaware) with your name and mailing address to:

Dr. D. D. Hook
P.O. Box 1682
Millsboro, DE 19966-1682.

Expect delivery within 6-8 weeks.